Jewish Sacred Music and Jewish Identity
~
Continuity and Fragmentation

Jewish Sacred Music and Jewish Identity

Continuity and Fragmentation

Edited by Jonathan L. Friedmann and Brad Stetson

Featuring the Notes and Reflections of
Cantor William Sharlin

PARAGON HOUSE
St. Paul, Minnesota

First Edition 2008

Published in the United States by
Paragon House
1925 Oakcrest Ave, Suite 7
St. Paul, MN 55113
www.paragonhouse.com

Copyright © 2008 Paragon House

All rights reserved. No part of this book may be reproduced, in any form, without written permission from the publisher, unless by a reviewer who wishes to quote brief passages.

Library of Congress Cataloging-in-Publication Data

Jewish sacred music and Jewish identity : continuity and fragmentation / edited by Jonathan L. Friedmann and Brad Stetson ; featuring the notes and reflections of Cantor William Sharlin. -- 1st ed.
   p. cm.
  Summary: "Examines the nature and significance of synagogue music in contemporary Jewish life, with special emphasis on Cantor William Sharlin"--Provided by publisher.
  Includes bibliographical references (p.) and index.
  ISBN 978-1-55778-872-6 (pbk. : alk. paper)
  1. Synagogue music--History and criticism. 2. Sharlin, William. 3. Cantors (Judaism)--United States. 4. Judaism--20th century. 5. Jews--Identity. I. Friedmann, Jonathan L., 1980- II. Stetson, Brad. III. Sharlin, William.
  ML3195.J58 2008
  781.76--dc22
                          2007043882

The paper used in this publication meets the minimum requirements of American National Standard for Information Sciences— Permanence of Paper for Printed Library Materials, ANSIZ39.48-1984.

Manufactured in the United States of America
10 9 8 7 6 5 4 3 2 1

For current information about all releases from Paragon House, visit the website at http://www.paragonhouse.com

Contents

Preface vii

Introduction xi
    Can Music Be Understood as a "Signal of Transcendence"?

Part I
Jewish Sacred Music
∽

Chapter 1 3
    A Philosophy of Jewish Sacred Music

Chapter 2 19
    Congregational Singing Past and Present

Part II
Cantor William Sharlin: The Making of a Cantorial Mind
∽

Chapter 3 35
    An Autobiographical Sketch

Chapter 4 39
    A Conversation with Cantor William Sharlin

Part III
A Symphony of a Cantorial Life: The Notes and Reflections of Cantor William Sharlin
∽

Chapter 5 51
    Set One: Continuity and Fragmentation

Chapter 6 . . . . *57*
    Set Two: Preservation and Innovation

Chapter 7 . . . . *75*
    Set Three: Sacred and Secular

Chapter 8 . . . . *87*
    Set Four: Past and Future

Glossary *107*
Endnotes *121*
Selected Bibliography *143*
Index *159*

Preface

Jonathan L. Friedmann

Cantor William Sharlin is one of the great figures in contemporary synagogue music. A rarity in his profession, Sharlin is simultaneously an inspiring cantor and teacher, virtuosic composer and pianist, first-rate scholar and intellectual. To use one of Sharlin's favorite metaphors, these are the many streams that flow through him. And just as proper singing technique requires the cooperation of breath and palate, the interlocking streams of an individual are necessary for the totality of his or her being.

Cantor Sharlin has been my mentor for the past three years. Once a week, I travel to his Los Angeles home to explore the mystery, history, and ecstasy inherent in synagogue song. As a teacher, he is hard to please, insisting that every note and every word be given full attention. He is known to stop students after each phrase, making them repeat it until it is near perfect, both technically and spiritually. He requires internalization of text and music. Sacred music must become his students' natural language.

Yet Cantor Sharlin remains remarkably warm and nurturing. Seeing his mentored cantors soar to vocal heights is a thrill that keeps him active into his late eighties. He reacts with deep emotion to well-performed passages, often putting his hand over his heart and saying, "You moved me." His love for music, his students, Judaism, and the sacred text is not well concealed. He is irrepressibly passionate.

Early on in my studies with Cantor Sharlin, he lent me a few of his handwritten essays. Through these writings, I found that his concerns for the cantorate echoed my own, and that he justly articulated what is often neglected in Jewish studies: the importance of synagogue song, both as a spiritual vehicle and as a means of preservation. I insisted that he lend me the remainder of his writings, some scribbled on hotel stationery, others previously published in academic journals.

Within this volume are essays written during Cantor Sharlin's long career at Leo Baeck Temple in Los Angeles. Some of his ideas are repeated, though with distinct nuance and detail, and I have organized the essays to reflect this thematic scope.

The major drawback of this collection is the absence of dates on virtually all of Sharlin's previously unpublished writings. However, despite this crucial omission, Cantor Sharlin's words remain timeless, and the issues he explores are still relevant to the cantorate. Whether written fifty years ago or in more recent days, these essays should serve to inform, inspire, and intrigue those interested in contemporary Jewish worship, Jewish denominational studies, the role and function of sacred music, and American religions more broadly.

Sharlin's career as cantor at Leo Baeck Temple witnessed the emergence of sharply divergent musical styles in the synagogue. In his writings, he cautions that these "alien entities" can pose a threat to the sincerity of worship, and blur both the necessary connection to the past, and the boundaries between sacred and profane. In an essay that follows, Cantor Sharlin sums it up: "Where there is no religious intent, it is the ordinary we bring into the synagogue—which ultimately brings the synagogue down to the ordinary."

At the same time, Sharlin understands the need to maintain worship as a relevant enterprise, and to breathe new life into ancient prayers. A prolific and widely performed composer of synagogue music, Cantor Sharlin writes new melodies for Jewish liturgy—vibrant and original—which somehow retain an unmistakable link to the past.

Following his teacher, musicologist Eric Werner, Cantor Sharlin contends that the debate over preservation or innovation in Jewish liturgical music lies in the mode of its assimilation: passive or active. With passive assimilation, trends of the majority culture are allowed to dominate the tradition, essentially replacing characteristic *nusach* (traditional chant) with contemporary and foreign elements. With active assimilation, however, the deeply rooted synagogue tradition is able to absorb outside influences, updating liturgical music for the times, while still upholding the centrality of Jewish roots. This is a delicate balance, and one Cantor Sharlin struggles to uphold.

This is but one of the many tensions that characterize Sharlin's writings. Raised Orthodox and later entering the world of Reform Judaism—as a cantor and professor of Jewish sacred music—Cantor Sharlin lives in two worlds. He is both fond and critical of his Orthodox upbringing, both in favor and cautious of Reform innovations. He stands between tradition and postmodernity, bridging the old and the new in his compositions and approach to prayer. He seeks resolution to the conflicts inherent within contemporary Jewish worship: sacred text against mode of transmission; spontaneity (*kavvanah*) against routine (*keva*); ethnicity against religiosity; and cantorial against congregational singing.

Complicating these tensions, Sharlin addresses the fragmentation of contemporary American Jewish worship, where rabbi and cantor share the pulpit, the liturgy alternates between Hebrew and English, and prayers are alternately sung and read. This notion is central to Sharlin's thought, as he contends that, "The religious spirit thrives on continuity; the secular invites fragmentation." To him, the fragmentation of worship is indicative of the breakdown of Judaism's traditional underpinnings, and an opening for what he calls the "mixed bag" of worship. Loss of religiosity allows the stream of worship to be interrupted, and for outside elements to enter the synagogue. In many cases, "true" prayer has become secondary to other, more practical, concerns, such as nostalgia, ethnicity, solidarity, and even entertainment.

Importantly, while presented in a Jewish context, the issues discussed in the following pages are not unique to American Judaism. The individualism and freedom of America have similarly caused tensions to arise within other religious traditions. It is thus my hope that Cantor Sharlin's words have use for Jews and non-Jews alike. The larger issue of religion in the postmodern world finds resonance here.

Introduction

Can Music Be Understood as a "Signal of Transcendence"?

Joseph G. Conti and Brad Stetson

After silence, that which comes nearest to expressing the inexpressible is music.

—Aldous Huxley

Music is a higher revelation than all wisdom and philosophy.

—Ludwig Van Beethoven

"Bach—Genesis, 1:1"

—H. L. Mencken

In the late 1960s, as American theologians and philosophers were casting around for a way to assert the relevance of religious belief to both a younger generation enthralled with all things new and experimental, and an older generation ridden with cynicism and scientism at the dawn of the space age, sociologist Peter Berger articulated a concept he called "Signals of Transcendence."[1] It was an attempt to take an inductive inventory of human experience, and on that basis infer the reasonableness of a belief in a Transcendent Being, a personal, intelligent, creator whose essence was partially and indirectly reflected by certain basic human phenomena and predilections. Signals of transcendence are "pointers," in Berger's words, "toward a religious interpretation of the human situation."[2]

The five such human properties or tendencies Berger noted were not intended to be a divine proof or an exhaustive roster of metaphysically suggestive human experiences, but only prominent, widespread realities indicative of the overarching gravity of human life and meaning, and their provenance beyond the merely human.

The first signal Berger notes is the observable human predilection for order and constancy, a sense of grounding of our experiences of all kinds in an order greater than ourselves. The mother reassuring an anxious child, the universal aspiration for a happy ending to a dramatic story, the recoil from anomie and anarchy, all speak to us of a benevolent constancy lying behind the vicissitudes of life.

Second, Berger presents an argument from play, the persistence of *homo ludens* (man at play), to step outside of the mundane and bracket our experience with reminders of the backdrop of joy. This demonstrates what Berger calls an "intrinsic intention" on the part of the human person gesturing beyond himself, and relishing if only temporarily what Berger calls "the deathlessness of childhood," a reveling that perhaps whispers of eternity.[3]

Third, Berger adduces the argument from hope, featuring the human being's propensity to be forward looking, relentlessly optimistic, and, despite its inevitability, announcing a refusal to death. This "no" to death is an idea Berger posits as at the very core of our *humanitas*, and indicative of the nonultimate character of our physical deaths.

Fourth, Berger presents the very unique argument from damnation as a hint to us that there must be more to this world than the natural and human institutions that fill it. Taking, for an example, the Nazi Adolf Eichmann and his atrocities during the Holocaust, Berger suggests that for some monstrous acts human punishment can never be enough, and that in fact the intrinsic intention of that punishment, at its core, points beyond itself. The grounding of our sense of justice and punishment must lie outside of ourselves, since we feel a depth of outrage at extreme human evil that we can never fully remedy ourselves, through our own institutions.[4]

Lastly, Berger sees the phenomenon of humor as gesturing transcendently. In the human paradoxes, absurdities, and tensions that give rise to the comic, we see the imprisonment of the human spirit in this world. And by laughing at this imprisonment, rather than by being overcome by it, the human soul asserts, existentially, that the imprisonment itself shall be overcome.[5] Despair is not the final word on human experience.

Can, then, music be reasonably understood as one such signal of transcendence? It seems clear that much could be said in defense of an affirmative answer to that question. We might first note, however, that the proposition itself plausibly could be seen as self-evident. So immersed is human history and consciousness in musical forms and experience that the burden of proof may well rest on those who understand music—and insist that it be understood—with strictly secular, material ideas.

Imagine, anyway, life without music. It is an interesting thought experiment indeed, to imagine a musicless world. It is also a terrifying imagination. The reduction of joy, the diminishment of expressive abilities, the subtraction from emotion that music-less-ness amounts to is unfathomable. Music-less-ness, is, in fact, one of the greatest sources of grief for the deaf.[6] Music is so integral to our human experience that we would feel less human without it.

We would like to suggest three primary reasons—or, more generally, lines of argument—why it is appropriate to conceptualize music as a pointer to transcendent reality. Our aim here certainly is not to articulate an exhaustive case in this regard, but only to introduce this possibility in light of Berger's influential paradigm, and encourage further reflection in that direction.

First, adding music to Berger's experiential roster seems *prima facie* reasonable because music itself incorporates into its structure and expression each element of the schema. It embodies the very signals Berger discusses, and so itself serves as a bright lighthouse on these temporal shores.

Music, by nature, is orderly. Scales, chords, progressions, the dynamics of tonality and rhythm have all been exhaustively categorized and classified by musicians and theoreticians of music.

Music theory—not to mention the conservatories dedicated to its application and study—constitutes a bona fide academic institution. Similarly, music in both its intention and expression, is playful. Not necessarily playful in the sense of unserious, but playful in the sense that it leads us out of the context of mundane routine, leading us to stand outside of ourselves, and also playful in the sense of calling upon other human skills and capacities to express themselves. And, of course, like any art form, music can express a range of emotion, including intense hope. The tension and anticipation, which a finely structured tune can wind up and then unleash in a climactic crescendo of energy and power, can very potently communicate and fulfill the emotion of hopefulness. After a long and finely crafted musical phrase that has broken through into resolution, one patently perceives the sense of hope exercised and fulfilled. In a similar if less direct way, music—through the devices of major and minor chords, as well the resolution or non-resolution of phrases—could be said to echo the imperative of justice. At the end of many religious prayers or hymns a sacred chord "Amen" concludes the meditation. That "all is well" and "it is completed" sentiment is a whisper of the human sense of justice, and the need we have that human experiences end rightly. The uncertainty and sense of incompleteness that touches us when a passage ends dissonantly, or in the minor key, makes this same point.

Finally, the humor a skilled composer or performer is able to convey through music is remarkable. Except for perhaps drama itself, no other art form is able convey the human sense of humor as effectively as music. The late pianist Victor Borge enjoyed a very successful career because of his ability to manifest humor in music.

A second reason to consider music as a supernatural imprint on human experience is that in the very enterprise which focuses on the transcendent, religion, music is utterly central. When humankind tries to consider and contact the divine, we turn to music. This underlines for us the surpassing import of music as a human faculty and phenomenon. As scholar Robert S. Ellwood wrote:

> Music is virtually universal as an important accompaniment of religion, except in Islam in which chanting and rhythmic recitation take its place. Music's importance in facilitating the basic task of religious symbolism helping the participant to make the transition from ordinary to sacred reality, is unsurpassed...[M]usic in religious worship sets the altered emotional tone and universe of meaning of the rite and does much to bring the participant into it.[7]

In a similar vein, Sir Jonathan Sacks, chief rabbi of the United Kingdom, remarks beautifully on the vitality of music in Judaism specifically. His careful observations are worth quoting at length.

> Judaism has long recognised the close connection between spirituality and song. *Az Yashir*—the Song at the Sea—was the first great collective tribute of the Israelites to God. Many of the Psalms were written to be sung, and the Levites used to provide choral accompaniment to the Temple service. To this day, music is the pulse of Jewish spirituality. We don't read the Torah; we sing it. We don't say our prayers; we chant them. We don't even read the Mishnah and Gemarah; they too have their special tune. Each text, and each period of the year, has its own melody. Song charts the biorhythms of the Jewish soul...There's a reason for this. When language is invested with deep emotion it aspires to the condition of music. As I put it once: Words are the language of the mind. But song is the language of the soul. That is why melody moves us in a way mere speech cannot. Judaism is a dialogue between earth and heaven, and when words become holy, they become song... [M]usic is the closest we come to expressing the inexpressible. As Joseph Addison wrote: "Music, the greatest good that mortals know, and all of heaven we have below."[8]

Third, in defense of hearing music as a signal of transcendent reality, we might note that few human experiences are as universal or as powerful as music. Even the most "tone deaf" or non-musically inclined person still has a favorite song, an appreciation for an anthem, soundtrack, or religious music in a manner that indicates personal intellectual and spiritual resonance.

Young children, too, manifest this awareness of the meaningfulness of music. From the calming power of a lullaby, to the educational assistance a ditty or rhyme can render, to the energizing consequence of an upbeat tune, children—perhaps the clearest and truest picture of human nature—intuitively know that music matters, that it speaks to us of our dignity and importance.

Along these very lines, there is an old story about the premiere performance of Beethoven's Ninth Symphony. Upon the majestic symphony's conclusion, as the long applause from the awestruck and uplifted audience reluctantly ended, it is said that a child in the audience turned to his mother and said, "What must we do now?" The child was so gripped by the beauty and force of the music that he thought he should respond with an appropriate human action. The music changed him and his outlook. It is, in fact, an ancient human phenomenon. In 1 Samuel 16:14–23 we read of Saul's affliction by an evil spirit, an affliction that could only be eased by David's masterful, inspiring playing of the harp.

Indeed, only recently has medical science recognized the therapeutic and healing power of music. Dale Matthews, M.D., a professor at the Georgetown University School of Medicine writes:

> Sacred music...seems to soak into our very bones, carrying the message of God's glory and God's love deep into our beings...Christians who have memorized familiar hymns, Jews who have sung *Torah Ora* ("Torah is Light") in temple when the Torah scroll is presented, and Buddhists who for years have chanted their prayers in the patterns of that ancient tradition know there's something special about participating in worship music. Singing allows us to engage our whole selves, body, mind and spirit, as we express our feelings about our God and our lives. Active participation in music can deepen the health benefit of worshipping God.[9]

Music as a form of psychological and medical treatment is well established with respect to various problems ranging from pain and anxiety during gynecological procedures,[10] hyperanxiety in general,[11] reducing the angst of women who've suffered physical abuse,[12] and to decrease presurgical anxiety in patients.[13] In many ways, the story of late-twentieth-century medicine is the story of the emerging awareness of the singularity of the human person, mind and body, and the capacity of even nonpharmaceutical means to aid health.[14] Surely the fact that music bears a healing and life-enhancing capacity for the human being is more suggestive of a physically transcendent reality than a merely physicalist interpretation of human experience.

It seems, then, if we consider music and *humanitas* together, there is an evident complementarity. Our selves and our lives seem meant for a musical accompaniment, amounting to an existential duet, as it were, wherein each of us plays our own part in the grand symphony of the spheres.

Part I

~

Jewish Sacred Music

Human communities throughout time have faced the challenge of preserving their own unique identity amidst the flux of relentless change. So much so, that the ancient Greek philosopher Heraclitus stressed that change was the only sure constant in the world. Now, two and one half millennia after Heraclitus wrote, the manifold centrifugal forces of post-modernity are asserting the power of change on all aspects of society, and religious traditions, in particular, are buffeted by their pull.

But those participating in religious traditions, and seeking to preserve their unique identity, are not without recourse. The power of music to teach, unify, communicate, and inspire is formidable, and the rich heritage of music in Judaism—a tradition well acquainted with challenge—is a primary exemplar of this effect.

In these two essays, we find a theoretical and practical exposition of Jewish sacred music by two practitioners and theorists whose devotion to their craft and people is complete and unreserved. The cantorial ministry demands nothing less, and in their words we find the intensity of commitment and reflection we might expect from those who lead the congregation into the sacred.

1

A Philosophy of Jewish Sacred Music

Jonathan L. Friedmann

Music is essential to the human experience. Despite its culturally assumed unimportance in relation to the issues of the day—political, economic, and interpersonal—the bond between music and culture remains unbreakable. Throughout the world's cultures, music serves as an identity marker, asserting the hopes and concerns of those longing to preserve ties to the past, and to retain roots for future generations. As ethnomusicologist Martin Stokes suggests, music is so significant that it "provides means by which people recognize identities and places, and the boundaries which separate them."[1]

History, customs, beliefs, identity, and pride—those elements that substantially define culture—are embodied in music, particularly music invested with a sense of the sacred. If maintained, such music can offset the ever-present pull of assimilation, perhaps the greatest threat facing ethnic identity in the modern world. At its best, the unifying power of this music amplifies emotional ties to community, both past and present.

Within the Jewish tradition, music's hallowed role has been preserved through *nusach* (traditional chant), *hazzanut* (cantorial art), and folk melodies—musical idioms specific to Diaspora communities, and cherished for their efficacy and authenticity. It is impossible to separate such music from the Jewish experience—liturgical melodies and soulful song elevate holidays and lifecycle events to their highest plateaus. Without music, the immediacy and emotional impact of such occasions would be strained.

This is particularly true of Jewish sacred music, which communicates petition, gratitude, praise, and exultation to God, and invites the Divine Presence—*Shekhinah*—to dwell among the worshiping congregation. Jewish sacred music helps separate the experience of prayer from the totality of existence, and thus effectively serves to demarcate sacred time and place. Sacred music of the highest order—that which is sincere, inspired, and true to the liturgy—is essentially sacred *language*: a means of communicating with God. For this reason, the Baal Shem Tov, founder of Hasidism, believed, "A soul cannot soar without melody."[2] Indeed, it seems that music is *the* way of prayer in Judaism. So, it can be said, sacred music is simply essential to the Jewish tradition.

THE ETHNIC-RELIGIOUS MUSIC OF THE SYNAGOGUE

Judaism is not merely a religion. Its self-understanding of *Am Yisrael* as the people of Israel implies that, without the Jewish people, there would be no Judaism; the disappearance of world Jewry would mean the end of this "people-religion." The Jewish people are an ethnic group united—with regional variations—by the cultural heritage of an ancient religion. Unlike the "pure faith" of Christianity, Jewishness is motivated largely by ethnic concerns—it is dependent more upon this-worldly cultural assertion than on the supernatural. Jewish ritual, customs, food, dress, and organizations collectively define what it means to be a Jew in postmodern times. And it has even been argued that, despite the decline of faith among the Jewish people, "the ties that bind the Jews are stronger than ever."[3] As sociologist Nathan Glazer wrote in his classic book *American Judaism*,

> ...even the loss of specific ethnic characteristics short of complete assimilation (the process by which we call acculturation), which to every other religion in America is—or should be—a matter of indifference, is of fundamental importance for the Jewish religion. Judaism is, in large measure, a historical creation of the way Jews have lived; while the way Jews have lived, and the way they live today, is, in large measure, a creation of Judaism. It seems impossible to divide the two.[4]

Like Judaism itself, Jewish liturgical music operates on two primary levels: ethnic and religious. Yet with this music, the *religiosity* of Judaism becomes central. The music serves to reaffirm the *holiness* of Jewish identity, an identity that is traditionally rooted in religion, but often operates outside the realm of the sacred. In the words of Cantor Jacob Beimel (1880–1944):

> The soul receives its very nourishment from these two attributes, religion and music. There has existed, since time immemorial, a strong and inseparable bond between divinity and the art of music....Rabbis wrote that the gates of song preceded the gates of repentance, and that the source of song is the nearest source of holiness.[5]

This profound connection between music and worship is by no means accidental. Both music and the sacred experience are at their core nonrational: elements of both can be explained rationally, but the totality of the experience remains ineffable.[6] It transcends human finitude. According to Rudolf Otto, the sacred experience constitutes an encounter with the "Wholly Other"—that is, "something of whose special character we can feel, without being able to give it clear conceptual expression."[7]

Thus, to *know* and to *understand* in this instance are two distinct things, as one can know intuitively that he has experienced the presence of God, but the experience itself transcends human vocabulary—it is by its very nature *beyond* explanation. To Otto, significantly, this awesome encounter is analogous to the effect of music. He writes: "Music stands too high for any understanding to reach, and an all-mastering efficacy goes forth from it, of which, however, no man is able to give an account."[8] Music is thus the ideal manner of relating the sacred experience: it approximates the qualities of marvel and grandeur associated with the Divine. The nonrational beauty of music, like the "beyondness" of the sacred experience, cannot be understood through mere conceptual analysis.

Music and the sacred are experienced primarily—if not *exclusively*—as emotions. The immediacy and impact of both transcend the realm of rational reflection. The sentiments aroused by music are not physical, but are the internalized—or "remembered"—feelings of tension, ecstasy, surprise, sadness, relaxation, and so on.[9] Like a symphony, the enormity of the sacred experience occurs instantaneously, allowing little time for one to decipher its particular elements. As an interviewee in William James's classic *Varieties of Religious Experience* stated, the sacred experience is "like the effect of some great orchestra, when all the separate notes have melted away into the swelling harmony."[10]

Yet, instead of confusion and disorientation, sacred music—as a blend of music and the "Wholly Other"—works to clarify experience. There is a force in the music that gives us a sense of the sacred, and it is felt more deeply than holy words. For this reason, wordless music is often as effective as emotive chant in communicating a sense of God's presence.

The power of wordless melodies is recognized in Hasidism, a movement within Judaism devoted to bringing *Shekhinah* (God's Presence) into the world. The use of wordless tunes, known as *niggunim*, was advocated eloquently by Hasidic master Rabbi Shneur Zalman of Liadi (1747–1813), who said, "Melody is the speech of the soul, but words interrupt the stream of emotion."[11] A *niggun* is endless, not limited by verses of text, allowing the singer's emotions to pour forth without concern for language.

Still, as is evident in the chanted prayers of Jewish liturgy, the words of a song can also inspire meaningful interpretation. It is no secret that certain musical qualities—timbre, tone, volume, rhythm, etc.—produce specific emotions. Our response to such music may be conscious or unconscious, yet we cannot help but be moved by it.[12] As certain feelings are closely linked to musical sounds—fear and trembling with low tones, awe and elation with sweeping melodic lines, etc.—the composer or presenter of a melody must use text as an emotive map, guiding him or her to the desired impact. Sacred music, then, represents emotional states, while at the same time inspiring the experience of the sacred. Perhaps this is why rabbinic tradition maintains that "any who approach God other than through singing commit blasphemy."[13]

Cherished liturgical melodies of the Jewish tradition stir simultaneous feelings of holiness and nostalgia within both presenter and listener. With these songs, the centrality of music in the Jewish experience is made clear. Within the enormity of Jewish sacred music exist particular melodies that transport the listener to another personal place, conjuring emotional ties to Jewish heritage and community. These prayer-songs provide an ineffable reminder of who one is as a Jew, and, as with all great music, begs for generations of repeat performance. As linguist Dwight L. Bolinger explained:

> Repetition, or the return to the familiar, to the learned, is more striking in music than elsewhere—a very good book may be read twice, a masterpiece of literature three or four times, a poem a dozen times; but in no other art-form could we expect the literally hundreds of repetitions to go on pleasing us. It is as a play-routine, with all the implications for pleasure gleaned from the habitual and the familiar, that music produces this effect.[14]

THE *KOL NIDRE* MELODY AND JEWISH IDENTITY

That certain melodies of the Jewish tradition have survived exile, persecution, and assimilation is a testament to the strength, durability, and efficacy of Jewish sacred music. Ancient melodies are inseparable from the experience of God, even after centuries of performance. The impact of such music lies in its ability to evoke the full gamut of human emotion, simultaneously fostering a sense of joy and sadness, elation and angst. Upon hearing the melodies of the Jewish tradition, one is compelled to feel the presence of the sacred—a nonrational experience of "going beyond" the ordinary. The most beloved melodies of the Jewish corpus convey intensity and spirituality, heritage and splendor, and the full existential range of Jewish experience. At its best, Jewish sacred music is a symbol of Jewish identity itself, able to shape and give personal and communal reality for the Jews.[15]

Among the various time-tested melodies dear to the Jewish heart, *Kol Nidre* ("All the Vows") stands as the most identifiable and revered. Its annual synagogue chanting, which inaugurates *Yom Kippur* (Day of Atonement), has become a major cultural phenomenon, bringing Jews of all stripes together in solemn assembly. The *Kol Nidre* melody is the centerpiece of the Jewish musical tradition—the gold standard in terms of form, function, and style.

Much more than a beautiful song, *Kol Nidre* effects a magnetic pull on the Jewish community. Since the advent of modernity and scientific rationalism in the nineteenth century, as well as the freedom and temptations of the Western world, many Jews, like many other religious people, have abandoned religiosity and rarely attend synagogue services. Yet on *Yom Kippur*, even nominal Jews crowd synagogues to hear the chanting of *Kol Nidre*, a pervasive phenomenon known as the annual invasion of "*Kol Nidre* Jews."[16] And, in Israel, it is customary for secular Jews to congregate outside of synagogues when *Kol Nidre* is chanted, even though they do not stay for the rest of the service.[17]

The power of the *Kol Nidre* melody lies in its ability to stir emotions and nostalgia. Attempts to decipher the difficult text are secondary to its capacity to move the listener. The true strength of *Kol Nidre* is, then, the actual melody that lies behind the text—a reality that accounts for, among other things, the popularity of Max Bruch's 1881 adaptation of *Kol Nidre* for solo cello.

Above all else, *Kol Nidre* is mood music: it establishes the atmosphere of repentance and introspection required for *Yom Kippur*. Austrian romantic poet Nikolaus Lenau (1802–50) wrote on *Kol Nidre*'s profound impact:

> …a song draped with the veil of grief; a night song dying away in the innermost recesses of penitent, contrite, repentant human hearts… Years ago I heard it [on the] Day of Atonement…the cantor began to chant that profoundly solemn and heart-rending song of absolution, so fraught with terror, and yet so rich in mercy. I struggled with an inexplicable emotion. I sobbed convulsively while hot tears poured from my eyes. Then I ran out into the night; my spirit torn and purified.[18]

This response articulates the passionate and inspiring nature of *Kol Nidre*, qualities further exaggerated by cantorial interpretation. When approaching a piece such as this, the cantor must aim for the mood, and the voice will follow. Sustained notes, dynamic swells, dramatic articulation and embellishments are common "tricks" used by cantors to enhance *Kol Nidre.*

What, then, is the text that has inspired this important melody? Strangely, *Kol Nidre* is not a prayer in the strictest sense, as it does not mention God. It is instead a call for the absolution of vows, specifically—though only implicitly in the text—between God and the individual. It reads in part:

> Let all our vows and oaths, all the promises we make and the obligations we incur between this Yom Kippur and the next, be null and void should we, after honest effort, find ourselves unable to fulfill them. Then may we be absolved of them.[19]

This proclamation is ideally suited for *Yom Kippur*, a day of fasting, repentance, and forgiveness. Occurring ten days after the celebration of *Rosh Hashanah*, the Jewish "New Year," the observance of *Yom Kippur* is mentioned explicitly in the Hebrew Bible (Lev. 23:27). Its proper commemoration requires that able-bodied adults undertake a complete fast—no food or liquids—for twenty-five hours, beginning one hour before the commencement of *Yom Kippur* eve. Jews are also forbidden to bathe, engage in sexual relations, or wear leather shoes—all of which are intended to diminish comfort on this day of introspection, and cultivate a spiritual cleansing.[20]

The ancient *Kol Nidre* melody embodies the impact of this solemn occasion and brings forth the penitence and praise required of the listener. But beyond this immediate purpose, *Kol Nidre* reminds the Jew of his link to the past. The *Kol Nidre* melody speaks to the Jewish heart more clearly than words.

THE CANTOR'S ROLE IN THE POSTMODERN SYNAGOGUE

In the context of Jewish worship, the presenter of prayer-song is the cantor, whose primary function is to chant on behalf of the congregation. Through the presentation of liturgy, the cantor expresses to God the collective devotion of the community.

A cantor who is devoted to the sacred text and the atmosphere of *tefillah* (prayer) is also an expert *sheliach tzibbur* (messenger of the congregation). The cantor has the unique responsibility to generate a prayerful experience, and to reinforce the congregation's emotional link to Jewish identity.

This is no small task: the cantor must be constantly aware of the link between music, prayer, and identity. He or she must approach the liturgy with confident humility, resisting the temptation of both prayer-routine and its opposite, ego-driven performance that seems to draw attention to itself. Indeed, to ensure that the cantor—as well as all who worship—embraces the tension between monotony and ego-satisfaction, the sages espoused the notion of *kavvanah*: correct intention in prayer.

Kavvanah in its original form means "to straighten"—to direct one's mind to pay close attention. As a noun, *kavvanah* denotes meaning and purpose, or "the state of being aware of what we are doing, of the task we are engaged in."[21] This is a central ingredient for the presentation of prayer, as the text and melody cannot be fully realized without sincere and impassioned singing.

The following powerful account presented by Martin Buber relates the total involvement of a cantor in the chanting of prayers:

> The soul lays hold of the voice of a man and makes it sing what the soul has experienced in the heights, and the voice does not know what it does. Thus, one *tzadik* (saintly man) stood in prayer during the High Holy Days and sang new melodies, wonder of wonders, that he had never heard and that no human ear had ever heard, and he did not know at all what he sang and in what ways he sang, for he was bound to the upper world, to the *Shekhinah* (Divine Presence).[22]

Crucial here is not only the all-consuming effect of the melody—the cantor's "soul lays hold of the voice"—but also the relationship between *kavvanah* (intention) and *Shekhinah* (Divine Presence), as the two are intertwined in the experience of sacred music. Spontaneity dominates as the cantor is swept away in the moment. The melody soars to great heights and the soul becomes "bound to the upper world," in Buber's phrase.

Binding to the Divine Presence is akin to what psychologist Erich Fromm saw as the "symbol of what man potentially is or ought to become."[23] Through genuine connection of text, melody, and *kavvanah* (intention), one gets a feint taste of the eternal bond to the sacred. In Jewish chant, then, the Hasidic adage holds true: "Within *keva* [structure] there must be *kavvanah*."[24]

To be sure, this ideal balance is not always attained, and the cantor—particularly within liberal Judaism, where God is not always a constant presence—often struggles against the realities of unbelief, both within him/herself, and among the congregation. Here, it seems, the problem of assimilation and scientific rationalism—hallmarks of American Judaism—impact both the nature and relevance of worship itself. Sometimes, today, the sense of holiness is largely absent; the pressures of postmodernity have inevitably challenged this rich tradition of Jewish synagogue music.

One of the difficulties of American religious freedom, at least from the standpoint of preservation, is the reality of choice. America stands as an oddity in the course of Jewish history. Where Judaism in the Old World existed within a dominant mainstream, American Judaism, like the bulk of religion in America, has come to cherish voluntarism. Denominationalism, personal tastes, and wide-ranging preferences have individualized a once thoroughly collective Judaism. For the majority of non-Orthodox American Jews—those who are active in liberal denominations or only nominally in touch with their Jewish heritage—Judaism is a voluntary and largely external component of their complex modern personas. Prayer rarely finds a place within this worldview.

For this reason, Judaic scholar Jacob Neusner sees that many synagogues are essentially "living museums" that preserve ancient rituals and prayers, as well as the liturgical roles of the rabbi and cantor.[25] To Neusner, this nostalgia for the past does not reflect the belief that prayer and ritual are essential to the lives of assimilated Jews, but rather that Jewish identity, as a result of its subjective and elusive nature, needs a formal, routinized external expression. As Neusner observes, "few [modern Jews] believe that supernatural salvation inheres in prayers, dietary taboos, and Sabbath observance." Indeed, "few pray. Still fewer believe in prayer."[26] In a way, then, the synagogue creates a periphery foundation in the lives of assimilated Jews unsure of their Jewishness. It often represents little more than a tenuous link to a largely forgotten heritage. As such, synagogue music has, in many instances, become a superficial expression of identity. The modern cantor must fight against these forces to sanctify the worship experience.

HESCHEL AND THE MODERN CANTORATE

Perhaps the greatest statement on the problems facing the American cantorate is Abraham Joshua Heschel's essay "The Vocation of the Cantor." This essay contains the richness and depth typical of Heschel's writings—it is brimming with invaluable insights into the importance of music in the synagogue. It is a testament to its profound and lasting insight that this short essay, originally a 1957 lecture, remains relevant to the contemporary synagogue.

In this essay, Heschel addresses the crucial concerns of the cantorate: the need for dignity, sincerity, and humility. His words eloquently express both the centrality of music in Jewish worship, and the need for cantors who are liturgically literate, mindful of their congregations, and properly oriented to lead the chanting of prayer—that is, driven by *kavvanah* (intention).

One of the central themes underlying "The Vocation of the Cantor" is the cantor's role in building a community of worship. As Heschel writes, "It is the task of the cantor to create the liturgical community, to convert a plurality of praying individuals into a unity of worship."[27] If effective, the cantor's voice acts as a beacon call to those gathered to pray; his or her *hishtapkhut hanefesh* (outpouring of the soul) unifies the congregation. Conversely, uninspired cantorial singing fails to grab hold of the individual *davener* (one who prays). This lack of emotional attachment to prayer and melody is disrespectful to the congregation; the cantor's primary role is to elevate the experience of worship, and to send the collective prayers of the community to God. Without the cantor's sincere focus on the text and chant, the congregants will likewise struggle to find resonance in the prayer experience. Without this connection to prayer, a sense of community will not fully materialize.

This is of particular concern, as modern Jews, consumed by the myriad demands and distractions of day-to-day life, are not inherently driven to prayer. In the words of Heschel, "The call to prayer often falls against an iron wall. The congregation is not always open and ready to worship. The cantor has to pierce the armor of indifference. He has to fight for a response. He has to conquer them in order to speak to them."[28] The pressure on this "conquering cantor" is immense: he or she must express a deep desire for prayer even when this longing is not present among the congregation. The cantor, through piety and inspiration, must *manufacture* an atmosphere of worship—the desire to pray must be contagious.

However, Heschel similarly warns that a cantor must not allow such enthusiasm to lead to narcissistic vocal theatrics. The role of the cantor is to lead in prayer. He stands before the Ark as a representative of the congregation, not an "artist in isolation."[29] Following his emphasis on the critical union of cantor and community, Heschel rightfully warns against alienating congregants with liturgical "performance." Mindful of the community, the cantor must chant in an inclusive fashion. Dignity, sincerity, warmth and beauty must be contained within palatable chant. An impressive voice is always secondary to the text. The cantor must be "humble before the words."[30]

Yet Heschel's thoughts on this matter can be taken too far. When aiming to foster a sense of community through chant, the cantor may hinder worship by employing over-simplified melodies. Such liturgical melodies, despite their accessibility, pose a twofold problem: they often misrepresent the text, and create a mood of complacency. As such, the popular "sing-along" melodies of the synagogue are often as spiritually harmful as the overly complex chant of the cantorial narcissist. When a prayer-song presents no challenge to the congregants, there is a tendency to sing the text mindlessly without reflection. The meaning of prayer is often lost in the contemporary repertoire, which typically resembles popular music that is alien to the Jewish tradition. Liturgical texts are often juxtaposed haphazardly onto "catchy" melodies, cherished for their pleasantness rather than their liturgical accuracy.

Much of contemporary synagogue music has its origins in the camp movement of the 1970s. The musical culture of Jewish summer camps was—and still is—heavily influenced by American folk music, and liturgical composers like Jeff Klepper and Debbie Friedman eagerly adapt this "American sound" to the synagogue. The influence of the summer camp style persists to this day, and a generation of Jews has grown up in this "new tradition."[31] To be sure, the popularity of these songs, and the coinciding emergence of guitar-playing rabbis and cantors, has its appeal, especially among casual congregants and children. But, as Roman Catholic mystic Thomas Merton warned, "Bad so-called sacred art constitutes a really grave spiritual problem."[32]

The embrace of synagogue music that is empty of tradition, simple, and enjoyable may in fact be considered "bad" as it draws our attention away from the activity of prayer. When there is nothing that distinguishes sacred music from the popular music of the day (save for the lyrics), there is a similar blurring of sacred and secular time and space, and a certain if unintended profaning of the religious-ethnic experience. Yet it is liberal Judaism's assertion that tradition must change with the times that has encouraged the free interpretation of liturgy into popular forms.

In addition, most modern congregants demand to participate in the presentation of prayer, and to sing liturgy along with the cantor. Unfortunately, this has resulted in the "dumbing-down" of the musical tradition, as the camplike "sing-along" atmosphere of the American synagogue requires that simple and familiar melodies be incorporated into the service. The melodies intentionally pose no challenge to the congregation, and emphasis on congregational singing has encouraged the seemingly unlimited interpretation of classical liturgy into contemporary song.

One can assume that the danger of this secular style is similar to what Heschel saw in his day: "So much of the music we hear distorts and even contradicts the words, instead of enchanting and glorifying them. Such music has a crushing effect upon our quest for prayer. One feels frequently hurt when listening to some of the melodies of the modern synagogue."[33] Ideally, new compositions for the synagogue should represent a balance between *nusach* (traditional chant)—the core of cantorial music—and musical styles relevant to the times. To be sure, this is the appeal of the music of Shlomo Carlebach[34] and others who bridge the divide between old and new. Their music has roots, and does not shift one's focus from the "Jewishness" of the prayer. They utilize Jewish folk and liturgical modes, while at the same time incorporating "popular" elements, such as pop music structure and driving rhythms. *Kavvanah* (intention) is preserved through an echo of tradition.

Heschel also points out that, just as one composing for the synagogue must be aware of the prayer's text, so too must the cantor internalize the liturgy: "It is not enough to know how to translate a prayer from Hebrew to English; it is not enough to have met a word in a dictionary and to have experienced unpleasant adventures with it in the study of grammar. A word has a soul, and we must learn how to attain insight into its life."[35] In many ways, the internalization of the text can solve the "problem of prayer." A cantor who is aware of the text in its entirety—recognizing the soul of each word—will quite naturally chant with feeling and nuance, emotion and determination. Even the simplest folk melody can become a powerful vehicle for prayer if performed with dignity and care.

This understanding recognizes the lack of impact Hebrew text has on secularized congregants, and sees the introduction of modern melodies as a compromise. Simple and "catchy" tunes are used to inspire singing and to entertain the uninterested congregant. So, as we've noted, contemporary synagogue music is selected largely for its entertainment value, rather than its respect for text or tradition. As one Orthodox critic of this contemporary trend believes, in liberal congregations, "by and large, the people don't know how to *daven* (pray), and so the natural solution is to make up songs."[36]

These songs, then, create a sense of *belonging*, but are less interested in a sense of *tefillah* (prayer). Indeed, many who enjoy participatory singing admit they are "unsatisfied and unsure if they had really been engaged in prayer,"[37] and feel that the perhaps less palatable *nusach* (traditional chant) creates a more genuine sense of spirituality. And in many cases, the "spiritless" nature of contemporary synagogue music is intentional. It is often the composer's ultimate intention to write music that congregants will want to sing, rather than to adapt music to prayer in a way that expresses its eternal meaning.

Lev Friedman, composer and song leader at Congregation B'nai Or ("Children of Light") in Boston, for instance, deliberately approaches synagogue music with the attitude of a pop music songwriter. Describing one of his compositions, Friedman said, "It just came to me one day. I may have been taking a shower. [I realized] this is a hit! This sounds good!"[38] Friedman does not mention a desire to write music appropriate for the prayer, but rather exemplifies sociologist of religion Robert Bellah's famous assertion that American religion tends to "[focus] on the needs and concerns of the individual."[39]

Yet Heschel is right to assert that Jews "have no holy music."[40] The melodies serve to enhance the text, and help clarify its mystery, but God—True Holiness—lies beyond the scope of the music. This mystery of God's "beyondness" should—if present in the mind of the composer and cantor—evoke attentiveness to prayer, and respect for God, the liturgy, and the congregation.

This seems to follow Heschel's warning that "words die of routine."[41] The text is eternally sacred—each repetition must be approached with reverence and sincerity. The mastery and love of sacred text is essential to the cantorate. Indeed, this is an area that all who lead prayer must develop. Without this knowledge and connectedness, the mystery within the prayer is lost, and the healthy sense of the *Mysterium Tremendum* fails to materialize. It is important to always bear in mind that "prayer is joy and fear, trust and trembling together."[42]

The cantorate today is in need of dignity, sincerity, and humility. The holiness of the prayer calls for dignified presentation; the cantor's voice must convey sincerity; the cantor's simultaneous awe and fear before God requires humility. Cultivation of these aspects will lead to a meaningful worship experience, and will allow the cantor to fulfill his or her central role within the worshiping community. And, with this sacred intelligence, for the Jewish community—living in a time when various centrifugal forces of society and culture threaten fragmentation—both ethnicity and religiosity can be preserved.

2

Congregational Singing Past and Present*
Cantor William Sharlin

I would like to reflect on the decline of the phenomenon of *davening* (praying) and its counterpart, the rise of congregational singing. Second, I will be dealing with the musical content of congregational singing during certain pertinent periods, examining its character and especially its role or function in the context of the larger entity of *tefillah* (prayer)—sometimes as an integral part of it and other times as an independent element having its own life and purpose.

I limit the discussion primarily to the nineteenth and twentieth centuries, first because we are close enough to the period that we can claim to be recipients of its synagogue culture, enabling us to look comparatively—past and present. Second, though we have some knowledge of the practice of congregational singing in limited parts of the service in Germany in earlier centuries, we have very little knowledge of its specific musical content until the nineteenth century.[1]

As an overview, it is not too much of an overstatement to say that congregational singing in the Ashkenazi tradition gradually enters a vacuum left by the decline of the power of *davening* and, in many places, its demise.

The general conditions behind this shift are fairly obvious: the impact of modernity, enlightenment, liberalization, assimilation, security in a free and open society, cumulatively leading to

---

* Originally published as "Congregational Singing Past and Present: Continuity and Fragmentation," in the *Central Conference of American Rabbis Journal* (spring 1994).

a decline in the discipline of *tefillah* along with the decline of liturgical and linguistic literacy and the rise of fragmentation in the very structure of the service—fragmentation of language, in that both Hebrew and the vernacular are used; fragmentation in the manner of oral expression, with reading and singing; fragmentation of the pulpit itself, rabbi and cantor—ultimately, a growing secularization of the very institution of *tefillah* itself, when in the deeper religious sense, *tefillah* becomes secondary to a greater need for communal, ethnic gratification and reinforcement of identity.[2] The religious spirit thrives on continuity; the secular invites fragmentation.

WHAT IS *DAVENING?*

Let us first look more closely at some of the prerequisite fundamentals that make *davening* (praying) a natural and believable form of religious expression, difficult to realize and transmit in the world of modernity.[3] When I speak of *davening* I do so in its classic sense—spontaneous, highly vocal, motivated by prayer as against a moderately vocal form that is culturally or ethnically motivated. The pivotal words are: the independence of the individual in a self-established state of privacy—an aloneness that allows no intrusion of consciousness. The classic *davener* (one who prays)—committed to *halakhah* (Jewish law)—is conditioned from childhood to pray in isolation. He masters the experience out of a strict discipline of thrice daily prayer—without freedom of choice—whether he is actually alone or in the midst of hundreds.[4] The *davener* does not need or require a synagogue—a wall anywhere will do. The qualitative experience of *davening* alone at home or in a *shtibel* (small house of worship) with a bare *minyan* (quorum) or in a *shul* (synagogue) of thousands remains unchanged. The degree of intensity may vary, but the dynamics remain the same. Even the intensive mesmerizing body movements we call *shuckling* is a vital ingredient that helps form a protective shield for the *davener* in the achievement of privacy—creating an illusion of isolation in the presence of others. I do not hesitate to add that the very character of the Ashkenazi pronunciation, especially in its penultimate accentuation, influenced by the Yiddish vernacular, contributes significantly to the fluidity of *davening*.

For the *davener* in the synagogue, the familiarity or unfamiliarity of the congregation is irrelevant. The *kahal* (community) is simply the necessary *minyan* (quorum) of faceless Jews.[5] Traveling from synagogue to synagogue does not affect the worshiper's concentration even though he may find himself in the midst of total strangers.

The *siddur*—the universally same *siddur*—is his anchor, wherever he may be. The singular unchanging *siddur* is his intimate partner in *tefillah*. But the key to this intimacy is a deep and loving knowledge of its contents. Without having internalized this liturgy almost as a mother tongue, *davening* would struggle to be.

As we observe further in the synagogue, we take note of an unusual condition that supported and reinforced the vitality of the *davener*—a unique relationship between him and the *bima* (pulpit)—that is, the *hazzan* (cantor). It is best described as a partnership in dialogue that allowed each to retain continuity in *tefillah*. The heart of this dialogue lay in the commonality not only of musical vocabulary, but of the very experience itself. Of course, the physical position of the *hazzan* facing the ark along with the *davener* crucially reinforced the commonality and prevented fragmentation. Because the *davener* was totally at home with the *nusach ha-tefillah* (traditional melody of prayer) of the *sheliach tzibbur* (messenger of the congregation), his *davening* formula was rooted in the *nusach* (traditional chant) itself. Of course, his chant patterns were based on the simplest elements—sometimes not so simple—but nevertheless rooted in its basic motifs.[6] One can say that the *davener* had a little bit of the *hazzan* in him, and the *hazzan*—if he were also a good *ba'al tefillah* (prayer leader)—would be a *davener* himself.

This unity in dialogue was strengthened even more by the improvisational spontaneity on the part of both congregation and *hazzan*.[7] *Davening*, in fact, is rooted in improvisation. In a *shul* (synagogue) of thousands, no two individuals would be *davening* the precise same pattern at the very same time. They may hear the sound of thousands about them without a conscious awareness of it. There is no such thing as unison *davening*.

It is in this unified environment that even the act of listening becomes integrated into the whole. Listening to the *hazzan* or *ba'al tefillah* (prayer leader) becomes a natural extension of *davening* rather than an independent act. It is as if the *davening* momentum is suspended rather than interrupted when hearing the *hazzan* singing—barring, of course, excess—and excess did and does take place.[8] All of this produced ultimately a rare *tefillah* structure that was self-directed—a leaderless prayer culture that has its own life and momentum.

Keeping all of this in mind, we now ask the question: What role did congregational singing have in this unique form of prayer? If it did at all, was it in fact congregational singing as we think of it today? Was there even a need for it? It is here that we again make a distinction between congregational unison singing that is independent of a larger entity of *tefillah* and that which emerges out of the total experience—in direct response to particular needs rather than as an end in itself. Parenthetically, I should point out that there are still many mainstream Orthodox synagogues in which congregational singing of any kind is totally absent—where "no-nonsense" *davening* cuts through the entire liturgy from *Ma Tovu* ("How Goodly")—*El Adon* ("God the Master")—*Kedushah* ("Sanctification") responses—right through to *Ein Kelohaynu* ("There Is None Like Our God") and *Adon Olam* ("Eternal God").[9] They simply have no need for group singing. When congregational melodies are utilized, they serve specific needs. The obvious occasions are the response to the *piyyutim*—liturgical poetry constructed in verse and rhyme. But even here, the practice of singing melodies was not universal—particularly on festivals and *Yamim Nora'im* (High Holy Days), when the *hazzan* sang and the congregation *davened* responsively. However (as in the case of prose text), when the *hazzan* reached a high point of intensity, a moment of emotional relief became necessary—a cooling off, so to speak, after the heat of *hazzanish* (cantorial) passion and pathos.[10] At that time a folklike tune engaged both cantor and *kahal* (community). This same need for relief through contrast, especially on *Yamim Nora'im*, takes place in liturgical prose passages as well—especially the more expansive and dramatic ones. It does not matter that the particular text sung to a folk melody might be considered even more desirous of emotional outpouring—more important is the instinctive need of the cantor and the community for a breathing spell in a remarkably spontaneous-like design of logic and form.

HAZZANUT AND DAVENING

Curiously, this group collaboration of *hazzan* and *davener* should perhaps not be classified under the label of congregational singing at all, because the experiential intent was still not one of joining together in unison singing. The *kahal* (community), of course, sang the same tune more or less; however, the individual *davener* still maintained his sense of privacy unconcerned with those about him, unaware of whether he was in perfect unison or even pitch with the larger *kahal*.[11] Oddly enough, a clear and precise unison singing might have an alien ring in the context of this "privately" *davening* culture.

The thread of continuity between *hazzanut* (cantorial art), *davening*, and melody was reinforced as well by the fact that the musical vocabulary of the melody was most often drawn out of the very fabric of the chant.[12] One can almost say that mere bar lines were inserted to transform the chant into a metric tune. Following the singing of the melody, continuity completed itself when the *hazzan* would close the text by returning to the *hazzanut*.

Another characteristic of these integrated melodies was their relative neutral design—lacking a sharp distinctiveness. An obvious and attractive tune would intrude on the continuity of mood as a whole.

At risk of overgeneralization, I would suggest that the extent of congregational singing in this context was dependent upon the relative emotional height of *hazzanut*. The greater the passion and pathos of the *hazzan*, the more the need for melodic relief for both *hazzan* and congregation. And, at the other end, the more the *sheliach tzibbur* (messenger of the congregation) sang as a *ba'al tefillah* (prayer leader) with simpler *nusach* (traditional chant), the less need was there for a contrasting metric melody.

All that has been discussed up to now regarding *davening*, and congregational song is specifically pertinent to the mainstream Orthodox synagogue in which the seriousness of the religious experience was dominant. However, one should keep in mind that there were periods in some synagogues when a secular thread entered more actively into the sacred—when the high art of *hazzanut* performed by the great ones with their supportive choirs served important cultural gratification.[13] In this context, the serious regular *daveners* would be joined by a variety of secularists and nonbelievers (many of whom still knew the mechanics of prayer), to satisfy their cultural needs. In such instances, congregational singing was reduced to a minimum, if at all, supplanted by the choir, which introduced more distinctive oddities of melodies, such as marches, into the larger compositions of *hazzanut*.

As we move into the new synagogues and temples emerging out of the various movements, we witness, of course, not only the diminishing power of *davening*, but its total elimination as well. Needless to say, in this open environment of assimilation and acculturation, many of the prerequisites of *davening* would either diminish or totally disappear.[14] Central to these prerequisites are the ability and need to pray alone as individuals, a diminishing literacy compounded by the effect of the fragmentation of the service: Hebrew-vernacular, spoken-sung, rabbi-cantor. Out of all this we see the beginning of self-conscious transition from praying to congregational singing.

One need not dwell much on how the radical Reform movement of the eighteenth and nineteenth centuries transformed the service totally, using the Lutheran Church primarily as a model, with virtually no Hebrew, cantor, or anything that remotely suggested the old tradition.[15] Music was placed in the hands of non-Jews, who often adapted church or churchlike hymns to be sung by choir and congregation. The hymn continued as the core musical content of the congregation right into the early Reform movement in the United States, but modified with a traditional overlay and supplemented with the remarkable persistence of the Sulzer responses.[16]

As an aside, one needs to be cautious in making judgments regarding the value of past worship content and character. We are prone to project the bias of our own background into that of another time and culture without realizing that what took place in the past, however different from our present way, constituted a complete entity that fulfilled the spiritual needs of the congregation, even within a more passive context. One must note here that, in its own way, the so-called classical Reform service, particularly in America, did in fact express a continuity of spirit with minimal fragmentation even in those fewer temples where pulpit was shared by cantor and rabbi.

When moderate Reform entered the scene in central Europe, the pendulum turned back toward the old tradition, but reshaping it under the influence of a disciplined Western aesthetic.[17] *Davening*, congregational singing, and *hazzanut* enter into a new relationship. The key impetus for the change was a rejection of the old free spontaneity of personal improvisation, to be replaced by a more controlled music based on the order and logic of modernity—specifically the Western aesthetics. And so, the dialogue between *hazzan* and *davener* shifted to one between cantor and choir, out of which emerged a new concept of congregational singing—a congregational singing now under the influence of the more dominant choral presence—while praying of a less personal expression receded into the background in a secondary role, in a quiet or silent form.

This emergence of the choir into greater prominence was not only due to the need for a more expanded art-aesthetic dimension, but was also a manifestation of a fundamental change in the very religious experience itself. In contrast to the past East European relationship with God, which was based on an intimate, personal, inward, withdrawal dynamics, mirroring the insularity of a *golus*-ghetto psyche—in a word, a relationship of immanence out of which the passion and pathos of praying and cantorial art itself were a natural manifestation, the direction of the Western religious experience opened itself up to the outer, universal cosmos, reaching out to an experience of a divinity on high—in the beyond, in a free spirit, in a relationship of grandeur and transcendence. For this experiential need, the choir, reflecting the general nineteenth-century style with its potentially lofty, soaring, and uplifting attributes, entered the synagogue.

SULZER AND MODERNIZATION

It is here that we turn to the world of Solomon Sulzer, the singular prime mover of musical modernization who single-handedly, out of the sheer power of his religious personality, transformed the chaotic musical state of a floundering reform process into a singular entity—inspired by his vision of the beauty of holiness in which tradition, divinity, art, and the spirit came together.

And yet, with regard to our subject at hand, one cannot consider Sulzer as a pioneer. Congregational singing was not uppermost in his mind. The lesser aesthetic level of a congregational mixture of sophisticated Viennese and growing numbers of Eastern Europeans singing together surely must have troubled his sensitive ears. His struggle to introduce the organ in later years was in part to neutralize and camouflage the idiosyncrasies of amateur singing.[18] Although Sulzer's primary focus was on the overall musical content of the service, it nevertheless did extend itself into a new concept of congregational song. Sulzer gives no specific indication for *gemeinde* (community) participation. Most of the choral works as well as the chamber music-like complexities would be inaccessible for the congregation to sing. Sulzer, like Lewandowski,[19] did not design his material with the congregation specifically in mind. However, he did compose numerous functional short pieces, which, though written for choir, were easy for the congregation to share—pieces that are more melodic in character. It is interesting that almost all of them function as "accompaniment" to special liturgical choreographic departures from the ongoing body of liturgy. I refer to virtually all the texts surrounding the Torah service, while the congregation is standing, focusing on another activity: *Ein Kamokha* ("There Is None Like Unto Thee")—*Vay'ehi Binso'a* ("And It Came to Pass")—*Ki Mitziyon* ("For Out of Zion")—*Sh'ma Yisrael* ("Hear, O Israel")—as well as other short "functional" responses: *Bar'chu* ("Praised Are You")—*Kedushah* ("Sanctification").[20]

It is of considerable irony that all of these melodies (modified in part), though surely of lesser musical import for Sulzer, have been kept alive until today in almost all branches of our synagogues, while the massive more "serious" substance of his liturgical works are rarely to be heard.

What is important to note here is that as radically different as the new and more formal musical content was, as compared to the informal folklike melodies of the old East European, the process of defining itself was the same in both, in that each in its own way emerged out of a fundamental mainstream that dominated the service. Congregational singing was not a fragmented appendage but an integral part of the larger character.

Unlike Sulzer, who had to deal with new beginnings and a changing heterogeneous congregation, Lewandowski came upon the scene in Germany, where the congregations had achieved greater stability and so they were able to enter more actively into a well-defined relationship with cantor and choir.[21] The congregation became well disciplined, being at home with the general choral culture and being able to sing well, in a unison choral manner, clearly designated liturgical elements fixed by Lewandowski, all in dialogue with the cantor, whose more formal and fixed *hazzanut* linked itself harmoniously to this singular entity of worship. Lewandowski, being more of a melodist, designed the congregational portions for ease of participation, but still echoing the general choral character. In addition, the orderliness and the accuracy of congregational singing were reinforced partly by the support of a large choir, but also an antiphonal formula where congregation and choir would echo musical phrases first sung by the cantor. Each of the three elements—cantor, choir, and congregation—was well practiced in its role. The essential point of it all, once again, was the achievement of continuity and a singular pervasive character that realized itself through much of Germany and was even explored in a limited way in some more liberal synagogues in Eastern Europe—by A. B. Birnbaum, for example.[22]

DAVENING IN OUR DAY

Here in this country, the task of identifying the direction taken by congregational singing becomes most complex because of the increasing diversity of synagogue affiliation—due, of course, to an expanding heterogeneous Jewish community coming from all parts of Europe and made up of varying degrees of acculturation.[23] What virtually all of these synagogues do increasingly share is an awareness of a need for greater or even new relevance in *tefillah*—to validate the institution itself in a modern society, unconsciously responding to a slow but sure shift from the need for prayer in the deeper religious sense to one that might satisfy more communal-ethnic, yes, secular, values.[24]

In this environment, the musical mainstream—in whatever form it may be for each of the divergent synagogue practices—begins to lose stability, becoming more passive, unable to exert influence during the search for a new relevance. It is here that continuity submits to fragmentation. Major efforts have been made to reshape the older prayer books, offering greater diversity in liturgical choice for the modern worshiper, but it seems, more and more, that long-range benefits have yet to be realized. As happened before, in dealing with this problem, efforts often turn to the musical content for solutions with greater congregational participation looked upon for the answer. And so congregational singing increases in the attempt to fill the void.[25] What follows then is reaching out—a grasping for song material drawn from *outside* the synagogue without necessarily having regard for its connection with some sense of the spirit of *tefillah*.

In those modern congregations, Conservative especially,[26] still linked to the old tradition, *davening* does continue but with diminished energy—partly out of a mixed assemblage of old-time *daveners*, ethnic *daveners*, novice *daveners*, and non-*daveners*, and partly because of the weakening of personal motivation and discipline. The dialogical continuity between *hazzan* and those who can *daven* becomes more and more fragmented—compounded by the increasing duality of the *bima* (pulpit), where the rabbi now takes on a more prominent role in leading the service: announcing pages, inserting commentary, and the like.[27]

The Young Israel movement similarly reflects the weakening of the inner personal commitment to *davening*, with its abundance of congregational singing. The very category of Young Israel, in itself, speaks of the growing need for *group* participation when the experience of individual privacy is harder to come by. The label at the same time institutionalizes the separation from the past generation of *daveners*.[28]

There are today, however, growing numbers of cadres attempting to revive and reestablish *davening* as the more dominant mode of *tefillah*, but it is too early to know whether these efforts will take hold on a deeper level, or whether they are still exploratory in satisfying more communal needs, perhaps to stimulate the spirit of *tefillah* rather than the result of an existent stimulus.

There are exceptions, of course, where greater stability and continuity do control *tefillah*, and here credit must be given to those individual cantors who, out of strength of commitment and influence, are able to maintain stability and, I must add, along with the help and good fortune of a compatible relationship with the other half of the pulpit—where both the *hazzan* and rabbi have a common systematic intent of practice.

In the Reform movement in general, in the 1940s and '50s, with temples attracting a greater East European membership, the practice of hymnal singing gradually disappeared, with Sulzer and Lewandowski responses still anchored in the service. But, at the same time, the so-called renaissance of synagogue music enters the scene when the focus turns more to the art of composition, requiring more professional singing and thus creating greater passivity for the congregational singer.[29] But we do need to keep in mind that the Reform movement, during this period as well as today, was not a single monolithic movement. We can still find temples today where some of the old hymns are sung, as well as some large temples echoing the old classical Reform culture with minimal congregational singing. As we move into our own time, we witness the presence of the greatest diversity in content and character not only of congregational song but also of the overall service itself, and diversity from one synagogue to another.[30] Because it is in the nature of things that, when a stable mainstream that reasonably controls the whole of the movement begins to weaken, each part of the movement begins to travel its own way, ultimately leading to a situation where the peculiar characteristics and idiosyncrasies of the individual participants, cantor and rabbi, now control the mainstream—reshaping it in their own image, so to speak. It can be said that a stable entity controls the participants while an unstable entity is controlled by the participants.

Very worthy efforts have been made to contribute song materials of higher quality that can relate more homogeneously to the spirit of *tefillah*, with limited results. Here, too, matters depend on the strength of leadership.

Because the secular culture by nature is impatient and lacks an ongoing discipline, it tends to reach out for immediacies, quick answers, often simplistic and trivial that require no long-range commitment.[31]

What are the sources of some of these new tunes? For me, the most curious one emerges out of the changing educational system of our children. Because our adult culture no longer does or can transmit whatever *tefillah* tools it possesses to the children in the old way—that is, through natural family exposure—the day schools and summer camps have taken over the responsibility by creating some form of a service especially designed for the young in which key liturgical elements are set to tunes that have immediate appeal for them—fun-type melodies as well as American pop. But somehow, many of these melodies found their way into the adult service as well, tunes most often having little regard for the form or the ideational content of the liturgy, tunes simply laid over the text—distorting them to no end.[32]

Ever since Israeli independence, a number of songs have found their way into the service, some of higher quality—the

Eastern ones especially—more sympathetic to the character of *tefillah* (prayer), others with strong secular associations that defy transformation into the sacred experience.[33] As lovely as *Erev Shel Shoshanim* ("Evening of the Roses") is as a love song, to sing it to the *Sh'ma* and *Echad Eloheinu* ("Our God Is One") of the *Kedushah* ("Sanctification") is no less culturally confusing than *N'kadeish et Shimcha* ("We Sanctify Your Name") sung to Mozart's *Eine Kleine Nachtmusik* in the old commercial synagogues of the Catskills.

We have also reached out to the table songs of *zmirot* (Shabbat songs). While some have proven to be effective for preliminary *Kabbalat Shabbat* ("Receiving of Shabbat") singing, even though borrowed out of another context, they are sometimes disconcerting when, for example, the *Shacharit Kedushah* ("Sanctification" for the morning service) is sung to Goldfarb's *Shalom Aleichem* ("Peace Be Unto You"—sung at Friday evening Shabbat services), a confusion of time and place. Another source from within the tradition is to utilize elements of *nusach* (traditional chant), but freezing them into a fixed melodic mode: the *Avot* ("Ancestors") or *Ashrei* ("Happy Are They").

In general, we see the dialogical concept of *sheliach tzibbur* (messenger of the congregation) and *kahal* (community) being gradually eroded not only from the musical standpoint, but from its liturgical foundation as well. Dialogue requires taking one's turn—it requires being able to listen; and it seems that the greater the fragmentation, the less ability there is to listen. It suggests a typical scenario when two people in a so-called conversation are speaking to each other but are not listening to each other—each one has his or her say but is not actually responding to the other. The liturgical formulas of leader and responses are ignored more and more. *Bar'chu et adonai ham'vorach* ("Praised Be the One to Whom Our Praise Is Due") becomes a singular congregational statement. In many instances the entire *Kedushah* ("Sanctification")—its introductory parts and responses—is sung by the congregation. The *nusach* (traditional melody) of the *Avot* ("Ancestors") is taken over by the congregation, freezing its intended free character. Of course, the very concept of *tefillah*, intended as a form of dialogue, is entering a gray area. To respond with *Amen* ("So Be It") is not enough.[34] Congregations, more and more, are joining with the cantor through most of the *berachot* (blessings).

The *Havdalah*[35] (service that separates Shabbat from the weekdays) liturgy with its contrasting elements is becoming homogenized into a secular neo-Hasidic tune. The formula of the *berachah* (blessing) as a personal expression is flattened out into congregational song. Listening to the other becomes more and more difficult. *Tefillah* (prayer), as an individual experience, whether one is singing, listening, or even reading, becomes more and more difficult to achieve. Being alone in prayer in the midst of others becomes elusive.

The secular, throughout our history, has always played a role in the evolution of our synagogue musical tradition; but to a greater or lesser extent, the mainstream was able to exert its influence on the foreign secular elements, assimilating them into the mainstream. But even when the secular material remained intact, unassimilated, the sheer strength of spiritual intent—call it *"kavvanah"*—could imbue the secular with a sense of the sacred integrating into singular continuity. Modernity—the secular—is with us. Whether we control it or it controls us is the question. The great Rav Kook spoke poignantly to the matter, saying that the old must be renewed and the new must be sanctified.[36] The struggle against fragmentation challenges the synagogue.

Part II

Cantor William Sharlin: The Making of a Cantorial Mind

Every artist is in some sense a product of his or her experiences. Those experiences, both historical and personal, external and internal, influence the outlook and behavior of the individual, as well as the personal expression of his or her artistic energies. It might be said that one cannot fully understand and appreciate the work of an artist without first knowing the artist himself.

So, in this brief section, we hear from Cantor William Sharlin himself, as he remarks on his personal and religious formation. In conversation with Jonathan L. Friedmann, we learn more about the experiences and attitudes that have sustained him throughout many decades of cantorial ministry.

In reading these pages, one is struck by the simplicity and humility of Cantor Sharlin, and the casual yet sincerely committed manner in which he understands his life and work. Though his remarks here are brief, in their plain straightforwardness, humanity, and love of God they suggest what would surely be—were we to hear them—the lengthy reports of inspiration, encouragement, and enjoyment from those to whom Cantor Sharlin has ministered throughout the years.

3

An Autobiographical Sketch

I was born Wolf Sharlin. I never found out how my name was changed to William—I forgot to ask my dad. In any event, that's what it is. I was born to a couple who came to the United States from Palestine. I was born in Harlem in 1920. I attended Yeshiva D'Harlem on 114th Street, and when we moved to the Bronx, I went to the Salanter Yeshiva. My parents were Orthodox—not strict Orthodox, but rather what we called "normally strict" Orthodox. My father pushed me, the youngest of his four children, to continue my yeshiva training into high school and beyond. My two brothers and my sister moved on into secular schools. After I completed Salanter Yeshiva, I had to travel back and forth between the Bronx and Washington Heights, where I studied Hebrew and Talmud at the Yeshiva University High School.

In the meantime, there was a piano in the house. My sister, who was about five years older than me, studied the piano—which was unusual for an Orthodox girl in those days. I gravitated to the piano, and I started to play, and my sister decided that I had some talent and interest, and arranged formal lessons for me.

In 1935, during the Depression, my family moved back to Jerusalem, Palestine—hoping and expecting to remain there. While there, I continued studying at an Orthodox high school, and continued studying piano with a teacher at the Jerusalem Conservatory.

Tragically, my mother died a year later in 1936, when I was sixteen. That hit the family hard. One by one, the family began moving back to the United States—my brother, my father, my other brother, my sister, and, finally, I returned to New York in 1939.

I continued my studies at the Yeshiva University High School. At that time, my sister encouraged me to enter the Manhattan School of Music. I was accepted, and that was the beginning of the turnabout of my movement into the larger musical world. But when I graduated with a master's in composition and piano, I wasn't sure where to go, or which direction to take. I sang in choirs, but I was not a formal singer. Still, I felt I had a bond to Jewish history and tradition, and when I heard there was the School of Sacred Music at the Hebrew Union College in New York, I contacted them to see if I would fit into some kind of a program. I thought I could train to be a music director for a large Jewish center because, in those days, they had major musical programs—that's what drew me to the school.

Once I was there, I took all the courses I needed—I already knew much of what was required—and I became attached to famed musicologist Eric Werner. Knowing that I had a rich background in Jewish studies and music—I even studied musicology—he saw great potential in me. I graduated the program in just two years, but Dr. Werner did not want me to leave. He was in touch with the Hebrew Union College in Cincinnati at the time and told me that the department needed me, and he arranged a teaching fellowship for me there.

Importantly, before I left New York, some of the people at the school told me I should study voice and become a cantor. So when I began my fellowship in Cincinnati, I started more seriously to study voice, taking lessons with some teachers at the Cincinnati Conservatory. For the three years that followed—the duration of my fellowship—I functioned as the music leader at the school. I became more and more serious about the cantorate, I worked hard, and began to enter that world.

At the end of the three-year fellowship, I was invited to remain permanently at the school as a professor of music. However, at the very same time, the president of Leo Baeck Temple in Los Angeles, who was also a member of the board of the Hebrew Union College, happened to be in Cincinnati. Leo Baeck, at that time, had a part-time cantor—not a particularly well-trained cantor—and they were looking for someone to replace him. So these two roads came together: I accepted a part-time cantor job at the temple, which in those days had only a small congregation, and I accepted a teaching position at the Hebrew Union College in Los Angeles. My career as cantor and professor began in 1954.

The membership of Leo Baeck Temple was growing—it had only 250 members when I first arrived—and the board of directors decided they needed to build a major synagogue. It was built on Sepulveda Boulevard in Los Angeles, and I became the full-time cantor.

What attracted me to the position most was that the rabbi, Leonard I. Beerman, knew of my background. That was a major force in allowing me to research and expand and bring into the life of Leo Baeck Temple both of my loves: tradition and music. I could compose music, and introduce forgotten gems of the cantorial past. I had a free hand in the expansion of the musical life of Leo Baeck Temple. Congregants often reminded me that the rabbi was the mind of the congregation, but I was the heart and soul.

While I was there, my name meant something, and I was invited for a number of years to synagogues on the East Coast and in the Midwest to be the "composer in residence" for a weekend. I would send my music to the synagogue in advance, I would rehearse with the cantors and choirs, lecture on this and that, and we would perform some of my compositions.

After a while, my schedule became too demanding—having to juggle full-time positions at Leo Baeck and the Hebrew Union College—so I began to scale back my work at the school, where I continued to teach a course in Jewish music to rabbinical students and introduce them to music of substance, which is often lacking in modern synagogues.

I have also continued to teach and mentor privately at my home. Some of these students over the years were very stubborn. They thought they already knew what they needed to know about cantorial art and the cantorial world. But as far as I'm concerned, there is never an end to learning. Even at eighty-seven, I am constantly being driven to the next step. I often ask myself, "Where do I go from here?"

As a singer, I've never stopped pursuing the possibilities of moving further ahead. Today, I am much freer in my singing than I ever had been before—I just open up my mouth and I sing. Reaching this level is the result of my constant, daily thinking and working on the craft, and I have benefited from what I have learned from teaching. I learn a great deal from communicating with my students. I have to first ponder within myself what is crucial to the cantorate, and then relate this discovery to the students. This has contributed greatly to my understanding of what it takes to be a cantor who is deeply committed to whatever he or she is singing.

I have also never stopped composing music. In recent years I have become a freak for the canon. The challenge of writing interesting and usable canons is very appealing to me. I am now working on a piece based on Rabbi Hillel's famous saying, "If I am not for myself, then who will be for me? And if I am only for myself, what am I? And if not now, when?" (*Pirkei Avot* 1:14). This last question "If not now when?" is where I am now. This is never-ending in me. I find myself learning and doing more and more, even at this old age.

4

A Conversation with Cantor William Sharlin

Jonathan L. Friedmann

Friedmann: Have the freedoms of America presented challenges for the preservation of Jewish identity?

Sharlin:[1] I was born in America, although my roots—through my parents and grandparents—are in Palestine.[2] I was raised as an American Jew with a deeply religious training, never having gone to public schools, but going to *yeshivas* (Orthodox Jewish schools) throughout my young life.

However, no matter where you are, if you live in another environment, sooner or later that environment is going to have some kind of influence on you. Without you knowing it, that environment colors your direction. As a result of that, American Jews have so many different shades of linkage with their Judaism and their broader universal view of life. Simply by living and mixing with another world, the dominant culture has the power to shape your identity.[3]

The first generation of Jewish immigrants from Europe came here and attempted—with some success—to maintain a linkage to the traditions of the past. But the second generation was born in a new environment, which enabled them to be freer to absorb the broader culture. In the Eastern European ghettos, where the first generation was born, contact with the outside world was minimal. But when they came to America and gave birth to the second generation—my generation—English, not Yiddish, became their language; *America* became their culture.[4]

Of course, depending on the depth of their parents' connection to Judaism—how strict they were—the next generation had different levels of assimilation. The individual lives of those in the second generation were closely embedded in their parents' beliefs and practices. That determined the different levels of how the next generation would find its way.

Then when you get to the third generation, anything could happen. You even find Jews who want to *believe* (embrace their religious heritage). They have discovered that their parents may have drifted away—something draws them back.[5] Others have little or no connection to Judaism, and have allowed their universal identity to dominate.

Friedmann: How was intermarriage viewed by the first generation?

Sharlin: This was very difficult for the parents of the first-generation. There was less intermarriage among their children, but there was some. That was a very painful thing for the first generation immigrants, who came from an environment where intermarriage was almost impossible.

In my case, my daughter married a non-Jew. I don't think this could have happened if my father were alive when she married. It would have been a terrible thing for my father, and I don't know what would have happened if he were alive—it would have been a very difficult thing. There are those who struggle with this even today. They see intermarriage as a major obstacle to the preservation of Judaism.[6]

Friedmann: Can you tell me more about your father's role in shaping your identity as a Jew?

Sharlin: If the Jewish identity is not deeply embedded, then the individual may drift away and find a non-Jewish mate or be attracted to other—perhaps Christian—ideas. Again, the preservation of Jewish identity has much to do with the parents' ability to instill it in their children.

My brother, for instance, when my father was still alive, married a Jewish woman who had been previously married, but did not get a Jewish divorce *(get)*—just a legal divorce. So my brother had to take his future wife to a court of rabbis to formally give her the separation so that they could be married.[7] That was when my father was alive. If that were not the case, I don't think he would have done that. We always tried to respect my father.

My father, on the other hand, secretly admired that I had moved into a different (non-Orthodox) world. He would occasionally say, "You could have at least been a Conservative cantor," but it was not a dramatic thing for him. After all, I was still in a Jewish realm—I was working among Jews.

He would sometimes visit me (from New York) at Leo Baeck Temple, but he would not walk into the sanctuary because men would be sitting there without *kippot* (skullcaps), and men and women were seated together.[8] That, in itself, would make him uneasy to even walk into this beautiful sanctuary. You see, beautiful sanctuaries meant very little to the "old Jews." All they needed was an Ark and a Torah, and that was their sanctuary. In the old days, that is all that existed in that kind of environment.

Friedmann: What is the main difference between past and present synagogue worship?

Sharlin: First of all, you have to begin with an understanding that in the content of the traditional synagogues of the past, there was basically no difference between one synagogue and the other—the traditional chant was fixed and existed in all synagogues.[9] There was something in common. The only thing that was different was that, in the small synagogues, there was a simpler chant of the *ba'al tefillah* (prayer leader). The prayer book was the same for everyone—unlike when we move into the present, where the prayer book itself has gone through changes.

Why the changes? Some of the answers are very obvious because we are dealing with a different culture in the synagogue today. In the past, you could walk into any *shul* (synagogue) and feel at home. The only thing is that, if there was a fine *hazzan* (cantor), he would do more elaborate cantorial singing, and the congregation participated in *davening* (praying). The chant itself was rooted in the particular chant the *hazzan* was using, but the congregation chanted in a very simple way. There was a dialogue between the cantor on the pulpit and the congregation. This was the unity of the past.

Friedmann: Is the attitude toward prayer different today than in the past?

Sharlin: There are many Orthodox synagogues today where the fundamental chant is still present. But the intensity of the inner heart, even in these Orthodox *shuls*, is not as intense today as it was in the past.

I go back into my personal past when I would go to [Orthodox] synagogues: *tefillah* was much more of a *living* experience. As one Orthodox Jew told me as we were talking about how Reform and Conservative Jews are trying new things to stimulate the congregation, "I do not pray three times a day for pleasure, I do it because I am commanded to." To not observe prayer three times a day leads to gradual change in the musical content. Without these internal roots, there is a need for external stimulation. When we do not *live* prayer, we must *manufacture* prayer.[10]

Friedmann: Do you think that this lack of internal religiosity is reflected in the way prayers are read and sung in the synagogue?

Sharlin: Certainly. For the most part, the manner of reading these texts is "just" reading, not expressing. I don't care what changes are made to the prayer book—in the Hebrew or translation—there are still ideas of belief, of Heaven, of otherworldliness. But the reading of these texts often sounds like *chol* (ordinary) and not *kodesh* (holy). When you do not have the connection, you are just going through the motions without an inner voice. You are stuck in the externals of identity.[11]

Because religiosity is absent, it allows the stream of prayer to go into the "pop" settings. Why are the people coming to the service? We have to give them something. We are not talking about deep feelings—there is an element of entertainment and participation. Not just sitting and listening, but the desire to get involved musically, so that all kinds of styles are introduced—even the lowliest musical content.[12]

During these sorts of services, nothing really happens. The music is instant, and they sing it over and over again. I often ask, "Why do you sing it again? Why repeat?" To make a statement. But when they repeat, they do it the same way each time. It doesn't inspire excitement, so one of the rabbis starts to clap his hands. And clapping hands is such a false way to get the prayer to do something—to touch people. If they are not singing, they must clap their hands. But to force people to clap and sing? I never allowed anything like that. Instead, I would often walk into the middle of the congregation and I would be honest and say, "I'm not quite ready for *tefillah*—maybe we should hum." I did this to bring the congregation—and myself—into the realm of worship.

When the "old Jew" walked into the synagogue he would pick up a prayer book and would right away be in touch with the feelings and traditions of *tefillah*. He didn't even bother to know anyone in the congregation—that was not important. Nowadays, in the Reform and Conservative synagogues, the rabbis can't get the people to stop *schmoozing* (chatting) when they want to begin the service; the people even chat during the service! It's terrible. It has become a community gathering of old friends.[13]

Friedmann: Has this "community gathering" setting contributed to the dominance of congregational singing in the liberal synagogues?

Sharlin: For one thing, today we have congregations that by and large are not in command of the language of the prayer book. The sound may be familiar, but the knowledge of the prayer is not. When you are *davening*, you have to be in command of the text. If you ask any Orthodox Jew, he can chant prayer from memory even without the text in front of him—there is an internalization of the text.

Today the Hebrew text itself is a foreign element, but the need to come together—to affirm one's identity as a Jew—brings congregants into the synagogue. What they do there varies today [denominationally]. If they come, what can they do? Often, very few passages of Hebrew are read, or they use transliteration. Even for those who have learned Hebrew, they are reciting it externally. They are not reciting something they can understand—they cannot translate the text in their minds. They are not speaking their own language.[14]

This cannot gratify those who come to pray or come into the presence of the community to maintain a link with their identity. So, congregational singing is a way for them to create an identity for themselves—to attach themselves to the tradition—even if the real inner feeling is not present.

The songs that they sing justify their presence in the synagogue. Whether they are in touch directly with what they are singing is relatively unimportant. That they are participating in this context is what is important.

One can say that people do not come to Reform and Conservative synagogues to pray—where the very idea of praying is of wanting and hoping. They are there to continue whatever link they have to Jewish identity.[15]

Sometimes I think of some synagogues as community centers with a Torah in the front. This does not mean that the traditions of the past must be lost. In the musical tradition of the past—with its potential for great spiritual value—there is a heart-wrenching quality that anyone can respond to.

I have given talks at churches for people who are interested in Jewish synagogue music and I improvised *hazzanut* (cantorial art) for them, and they were in awe. They were aware that something was happening in me—I was not just demonstrating. There is great beauty in the chant; there is heart and soul. The text is inside of me. I do not have to think about the words— it is my natural text. It is of great value to have the text memorized and internalized so that you can lose yourself in the piece you are singing.

I have emerged out of a very Orthodox background, which is, in a way, a blessing for me because I've internalized that whole world even though I am living in a different world. I can fuse the two worlds together and I know that when I sing *hazzanut*, even in my Reform synagogue, I know that there are many people who are moved by what I do—I want to emotionalize them. They open themselves up more. I find that to be a good device to bring them into what is normally a strange or foreign entity.

Friedmann: How can secularized Jews be brought back into the synagogue?

Sharlin: The fact that the cultural element of the synagogue—as opposed to the religious—has become so dominant makes it possible to be involved in the synagogue without having to struggle with religious questions. This is attractive for those who still have a hint—or in many cases a stronger sense—of identity as Jews. They are on the borderline of forgetting about their Jewish heritage—they want to keep their identity alive, and really, the only way is through the synagogue.[16]

The American synagogue, as it was evolving, made it easier for them because they didn't have to come into an Orthodox environment, which required commitments of behavior and belief. They could be comfortable. The music was already "Americana," or at least half Jewish, half American in style. The synagogue functioned as an easy transition from the secular to the sacred—it was not challenging.

It is more difficult to shed oneself of both conscious and unconscious memories of Judaism. Giving up Jewish identity altogether—as some have[17]—is a radical and powerful thing. No matter how far one drifts away into the universal frame of mind, there is always a glimpse of the inner life.

Friedmann: During your time at Leo Baeck Temple, did you notice that people were drawn to the "universalist" atmosphere of the services?

Sharlin: Many who joined Leo Baeck [in Los Angeles] would not have joined any other temple because we had a rabbi who was as much a universalist as he was a Jew.

I was once attending a rabbinic conference, and there was a discussion amongst the rabbis having to do with which way they were leaning: univeralist or traditionalist. The head rabbi of the New York School of Hebrew Union College was standing next to me. He asked me, "My goodness, what's going on?" I said, "Some are drawn more to a universal need, some more to their identities as Jews."

I saw this division among rabbinic students when I studied at the Hebrew Union College. I was friendly with both sides—I was fluent in the traditional ways, and I was living in the modern realm. But I had more friends who were universalists because of their love of music.

Friedmann: Do you bring your life in the old and new worlds together in your liturgical compositions?

Sharlin: Yes. I live in the world of the past, but I am also one of the few cantors who has studied composition in modernity.[18] There are times when my composition touches upon, unconsciously, my internal knowledge of synagogue music. But even when I move away and into a style of composition—more modern—I feel there are elements of the tradition still present. When I think about something for the synagogue, my mind unconsciously focuses on the way music reaches out to higher places—to elevation. That is the key.

You can do any kind of service if the motivation is to reach up into higher places—to elevate yourself. This is the central goal, as opposed to filling time with "just" singing. Even if you do something of a pop nature, there is a possibility of reaching into a higher place—of instilling it with a feeling of *tefillah*.[19] But that is very rare to find. What happens too often is that songs are repeated, and there is a hesitancy to teach a musical composition to a congregation that takes more than a few times to master. There are few pieces used of high inner beauty.

I worked with rabbinic students at the Hebrew Union College for many years, and I would introduce my melody for *Ahavah Rabbah* ("With Abounding Love") to them. The familiar melody bothered me because it struggles against the content of the text; the composer just threw a melody on the text. The average congregation does not know the difference. I introduced my piece to the rabbinic students and I didn't expect them to learn it right away. I was not expecting what so often happens today: instant mastering of simplistic melodies repeated without change.

Why do you repeat something? Because you are trying to make a point—if you want to repeat something, you can intensify the harmonic color to help justify repetition.[20] Also, hand clapping along with the prayer-song has become a thing, but I have found that congregants often get tired because they are not clapping out of an intense need, which, incidentally, was a part of Hasidic tradition. The Hasidim rarely clapped their hands, but when they did it was because they reached such a high level of intensity that they needed to clap to add something else. How does a cantor stimulate that feeling? By communicating his or her spirit and soul.

Friedmann: What is your attitude toward "pop" music in the synagogue?

Sharlin: The likelihood is that in order to attract the younger generation, this music will remain an attractive option. This music originated in youth summer camps, where all kinds of simplistic songs are created that by and large do not require real musicality—they are songs that can be picked up in a short amount of time; they do not need to be *learned*.[21]

This music has come back to the community. When we are dealing with the Reform congregation, there is a predominance of adults who do not remember the musical traditions of the past.

I do, however, find them linking themselves with the *Kol Nidre* ("All the Vows") melody of *Yom Kippur* (Day of Atonement) evening. This is partly because it happens only once a year. The less often there is an experience of something, the more there is a possibility of wanting to keep it. The *Kol Nidre* ("All the Vows") plays that role. It is not necessarily a beautiful piece of music, and it has very little to do with the text, but it is the first thing that is done on *Yom Kippur* evening. The less an event happens during the year, the more even Reform Jews seek to do what is more traditional—they want to hear the *Kol Nidre*. Also, what is happening is that many Reform Jews want to have traditional funerals. There is a need for them to make this time of grief and uncertainty more "official."[22]

Friedmann: Do you find that the synagogue music of the past can enhance one's attachment to Jewish identity?

Sharlin: Yes. It has to do with an emotional attachment to Judaism. Here we are talking about *identity*, not necessarily practice. When we look at Reform Jews, many of them do not follow *kashrut* (dietary laws) or other Jewish laws, but they never fully relinquished their link with their identity as Jews. The music is a way for them to become emotionally attached. Some will say, "That reminds me of the old days." This is one of the reasons why traditional music of the past is so important: it connects us to our history.

Friedmann: What are the elements of synagogue music from the past that should be preserved?

Sharlin: It depends on the person who is chanting. Song leading is a religious experience. You must make the song beautiful, even if it is not obviously beautiful. You have to cultivate a deep feeling for the text. But often the song leader just sings a tune with words, and very often the tune does not have anything to do with the text. The cantorial tradition is not merely a collection of melodies.

Part III

A Symphony of a Cantorial Life: The Notes and Reflections of Cantor William Sharlin

It is a characteristic of the committed professional that he manifests a concern for the integrity of the craft itself, in which he participates. He strives for excellence, but also exercises a sense of ownership over the enterprise itself, knowing that the work is more important than his own reputation or egocentric needs. For the artistic craftsman, his vocation is not merely "work" or a "career," but a living endeavor, a disciplined practice that must thrive and function, far beyond the professional's own participation in it.

In this series of reflections and comments from Cantor Sharlin—written over many years often as informal observations—he engages a wide range of topics, but always with an eye for what is best for the congregation, what best reflects Jewish tradition, and what is best for the institution of the cantorate, knowing that institution is so central to the sustaining of Judaism's identity.

We encounter in these passages an active mind and concerned heart, engaging issues of the cantorate and Jewish life in general with the honesty and intellectual acuity that has characterized Cantor Sharlin's service to his people.

5

Set One: Continuity and Fragmentation

1. JEWISH IDENTITY

Preservation of Jewish identity is partially motivated by love of the past—to lose identity means leaving oneself bereft of a past. While losing one's past may be liberating for some, it may also represent a forbidden emptiness with only an unknown future ahead. Where there is less and less knowledge of the past, assimilation becomes more and more possible; the trauma of the loss of the past is no longer a factor.[1] Attachment to the past, of course, varies in degree and intensity.

Some experience the past deeply, as far back as Sinai, if not Abraham. Some experience it as the pathos of the Diaspora struggle for survival. Others link themselves back only to Hitler and Auschwitz.[2] And we tend to overlook that for many people, the only link to the past is a grandparent.

These dimensions of Jewish self-understanding today have less to do with being comfortably Jewish and more to do with being comfortable as surface Jews—we experience ourselves as less distinctly Jewish. We want to remain Jews, but most of us do not know how to foster our connection with Judaism.

2. COMPOSERS OF SYNAGOGUE MUSIC

Never before in the history of the synagogue have we witnessed such a vast diversity of musical content as we do today. And never before have these sharply divergent styles entered the synagogue at such a rapidly ongoing pace.

Of course, some of the reasons might be obvious. In the past, the presence of a strong stable tradition (a mainstream) in ghettoized and unassimilated Diaspora communities required relatively little musical departure, and even when new musical ideas entered the synagogue, they were absorbed into the mainstream, making the changes hardly recognizable.[3]

Today, as a result of the increasing weakness or even absence of a mainstream tradition, the synagogue has left itself wide open for almost anything and everything that seeks to enter the vacuum.[4] What may be less obvious are two underlying conditions: one having to do with a shift in the basic function of music in worship in the past and in the present, and the other dealing with who were and who are now the composers who contribute to synagogue music.

With regard to function, in the past the musical traditions and the changes they underwent were motivated and inspired by a preexistent passion and need for prayer itself, and so the changes that took place were simply an expansion of the old. And the new entered this same creative process stimulated by the ever-present energy of *tefillah* (prayer). Change was hardly recognizable.

Today the opposite is the case. Because the inner need for personal prayer has so diminished or is absent altogether,[5] the function of music is an attempt to stimulate the inclination to pray, or at least to create a prayerful environment into which we may enter.

When the purpose of music is to stimulate prayer, it invites ongoing exploration and experimentation. When music is looked upon to solve the problem of prayer rather than to enhance it, we tend to try all kinds of possibilities.

So, who is responsible for the creation of the many varied and divergent styles of music? Who were the composers in the past and who are they today?

The answer lies in the concept of insiders and outsiders. In the past in Eastern Europe the composer was always an insider, that is, a *davener* (one who prays), and *hazzan* (cantor) whose creativity was driven by a deep intimacy with the liturgical and musical tradition. The old was ever-present as it was expanded, and foreign elements were digested and Judaized by the old. Change was slow and virtually unrecognizable.[6]

In the past, the *hazzanim* (cantors) were the creators: likeminded entities in almost every synagogue in Eastern Europe rooted in the same old tradition. Today, however, it is precisely the diversity of background and musical personalities of the many contemporary composers that contribute directly to the mixed-bag character of liturgical music.[7]

There are some—a minority—who are insiders with some link to tradition, and perhaps even to the very experience of prayer. The emotional dimension of *tefillah* is reflected in their music. Then we have those who are both insiders and outsiders. While they may have the knowledge of the tradition, they may make use of it in a more detached way because they are outsiders to the inner experience of prayer. They are guided primarily by aesthetic needs or secular-ethnic attitudes.

As we move into the outside we may find a small category of composers for whom tradition is totally foreign but who are nevertheless moved by a spiritual impulse. It is here that the world of pop enters the scene—these are the complete outsiders whose only natural musical milieu is the culture of pop, and who most often come to the synagogue via the camp experience.[8]

Composers from all of these categories contribute to the mixed multitude—a conglomeration of every conceivable mode and style. If one were to cull out of all of this a principle, it would be this: When a tradition is stable and vibrant, it controls and dominates the individual participants, and when the mainstream is weak with little or no influence, it is the individual composer, cantor, and rabbi who controls and dominates ongoing change.

3. LISTENING TO THE PULPIT

During a course on synagogue music for rabbinic students, I presented various liturgical compositions. The students listened to one particular piece and responded most positively; some were touched. Then one student commented with a troubled mind that, although it was moving, he questioned its use in a service because the congregation would listen to it and not participate; just listening would distract congregants from the vocal act of prayer.

What was especially intriguing was that the student was touched by the piece, yet had to reject it as a part of the worship service. Was the apparent contradiction due to the student's ability to accept, or *submit* to, a listening experience in the classroom, but when he projected himself into the sanctuary service, he had to reject it? Was it that listening had little or no function in active worship? Or even worse, was it that he reacted out of a mind-set of a future rabbi on the pulpit? It seemed to me that his concern emerged from two rather simplistic and dubious equations: in prayer, vocal participation equals experience, and listening equals passivity.[9]

We need to examine underlying conditions to help explain the above contradiction; those conditions may illuminate the direction of synagogue music and may explain why some fear that we may be witnessing the decline of the cantorate.

I approach such probing from the mind-set and vested interest of a cantor, but a vested interest that extends beyond such externals as title, training, past history, and preservation. My vested interest emerges from a deep conviction that as cantors, we still possess that which can elevate the spirit of a congregation in prayer. I honestly believe that what we can offer is worthy of experiential listening. And so I turn to inner listening, particularly in light of growing tendencies to disparage it in prayer, as some believe such listening inhibits congregational participation and breeds passivity—a notion that itself inhibits listening.

Congregational participation in song is, of course, important in engaging the spirit, but when congregational leaders consider participation as the alternative to "just" listening, we have simplistic reasoning. When "just" listening is singled out as *the* problem in worship and congregational singing as *the* solution, we brush aside critical questions: Is "just" listening the only kind? Is active, experiential listening possible? If so, what are the prerequisites? What conditions stimulate or inhibit active, experiential listening?

The two entities in worship, the congregation and the pulpit, need to exist in a state of unity and share a commonality of experience, a dialogue of the spirit, uninterrupted continuity of the sacred. The pulpit was historically occupied by one individual—the *hazzan*—in dialogue with a congregation made up of individual worshipers, each of whom entered with *siddur* (prayer book) in hand.[10] Such a one-on-one relationship fostered greater *kavvanah*[11]—spiritual focus or prayerful state—an undisturbed conversation between the *hazzan* and the individuals in *kahal* (community). As *hazzan* and *kahal* faced the Ark (holding the Torah), active *davening* and active listening both formed part of a single fabric of prayer.

As we move into the modern synagogue, with the pulpit occupied by two or more presenters, we face potential fragmentation—a diffused focus that extends beyond obvious external differences: visual presence, voice, personality, style, alternation of Hebrew and English, shifts between reading and singing. These realities in themselves can limit involvement, unless these disparate activities can be transcended, merged in a single spiritual stream, a unity of experiences emanating from the pulpit. When the pulpit breaks up into unrelated parts, it separates itself spiritually from the congregation, which then interferes directly with inward listening. Experiential listening requires oneness of intent on the part of the rabbi and cantor. This unified atmosphere diminishes self-consciousness; the different parts become a whole so that listening is no longer an activity but rather an integral part of a single, sacred entity. Spiritual unity in the pulpit can establish an environment for spiritual listening.

We should be careful with terms that are often thrown about loosely: worship and prayer. When the core meaning of these words is disconnected from a deep sense of the sacred, we may unknowingly exploit sacred text to further secular Jewish needs or reinforce ethnic identity.[12]

The more fragmented the pulpit, the more passive the listener, the greater the experiential unity of the pulpit, the deeper is experiential listening. Spiritual unity on the pulpit establishes an environment for spiritual listening. Under the best conditions, listening can be an integral part of prayer rather than an interruption.

Should the pulpit's experience be no less than what it wishes for the congregation? Can the pulpit affect a prayer experience when it is itself outside of it?

6

Set Two: Preservation and Innovation

4. FROM SINAI

Moses received the Torah at Sinai and transmitted it.[1] It is surely the power of this very idea of receiving and transmitting that has carried us through the centuries to this day. Yet it is more than the act itself. Were it not for the remarkable passion and love for that which has been transmitted and the drive to pass it on with love, would we still be here? And so it has been written and prayed: We ask the Compassionate One to enable our hearts to hear, to learn, to teach.[2]

To hear with open hearts as well as minds so that we may be moved to recognize with wonderment the miracle of our tradition, to learn with endearment and thankfulness, and to be able to teach in the loftiest sense: to transmit not only the words of instruction, but the love as well. And so may we learn that what we teach does not come from us but *through* us.

5. THE STATIC AND DYNAMIC IN SYNAGOGUE SONG

The role of music in the synagogue has often been identified with poetic clichés: "Sing unto the Lord a new song"[3]; "Music is the language of the gods"[4]; "Song lifts our prayers unto the heavens."[5] These are beautiful thoughts—important, and inspirationally valid in the wonderful realm of experience.

There has been, however, another significant aspect of our musical tradition, more practical perhaps, that has played a vital role in the process of preservation, of worship, of the traditional *siddur* (prayer book), and perhaps even of the synagogue itself.

Throughout the evolution of our tradition there have always existed two opposite streams flowing through our religious life. One is the sacred word; the other is the "play" on the sacred word. The sacred word—the stable stream—can be described as fixed, untouchable, unchanging, rigid, static. On the other hand, the stream of the "play on words" can be described as free, creative, ever changing, dynamic.

These two opposing streams of the static and dynamic, coexisting, and interplaying with each other, have served as the perfectly balanced ingredients to support the process of preservation. The unchanging fixed word is the anchor—the free play element embellishes and stimulates the fixed word, but does so without tampering with it or modifying its original substance.

Should the sacred word submit itself to change, it would eventually lose its stability and, even worse, its credibility. On the other hand, if the dynamic ingredient would not impose itself on the static, the sacred word, while remaining intact, would soon become stagnant, petrified, a relic of the past.[6]

This harmonious duality can be seen functioning in both Scripture and the prayer book. Our rabbis of the past were obsessive in controlling every word and every syllable of the Bible from revision—from *any* change. Yet they accepted, however unhappily, considerable and ongoing freedom in the interpretation. The ingenious and imaginative literature of the Midrash ("Exegesis"),[7] Agaddah ("Narration"),[8] and commentaries imbued the rigid text of the Bible with constant vitality—the dynamic elevates the static.

In the very same way, the ever-changing music of the synagogue, throughout our history, helped breathe into the fixed text of the *siddur* a new life and energy, liberating it from stagnation. The inflexible rule in the development of the *siddur* liturgy stated simply: once a prayer entered the *siddur* it could not be deleted or changed.[9] One might add to it new texts, but never remove or alter its original content.

Still, the evolution of our synagogue tradition enjoyed an enormous freedom that enabled it to both energize the old text and at the same time help preserve its original entity. The dynamic preserves the static without changing it.

What about this musical freedom? Throughout our history and especially in the Ashkenazi (European Jewish) tradition, wherever and whenever our people found themselves, they brought into the synagogue musical elements out of their Diaspora environments, thus constantly affecting the character of whatever the existent musical mainstream was at any given period.[10] There were times when hardly anything was off limits: peasant songs, folk songs, street songs, military marches, and, on some rare occasions, even church hymns found their way into the synagogue.

6. ACTIVE AND PASSIVE ASSIMILATION*

There exists a heterogeneous accumulation of radically varied musical pieces that have in one way or another entered the synagogue of today. Of course, each individual synagogue would likely stress only some of these varied styles and forms. The particular stress would, naturally, first depend on whether the synagogue is Orthodox, Conservative, or Reform; but equally important, the choice of musical content would depend on the distinct character or personality of each congregation—the socioeconomic, cultural, and even ethnic background of its members—all the way down to the particular bent, prejudices, abilities, limitations, and idiosyncrasies of the cantor, musical director, and oftentimes the rabbi.

The largest number of diverse pieces come from the past one hundred years—a result of the emerging freedom of the *Haskalah* (Enlightenment), liberalization of the synagogue, and assimilation.[11] Indeed, the most radical experimentation and departures have entered the synagogue in only the past decade or two—a period when the musical mainstream had reached a total breakdown.

---

* This paper was presented following a "musical service" at Leo Baeck Temple, which explored musical settings of the liturgy from various regions, periods and movements.

It is this important concept of mainstream in constant flux that I wish to discuss as my central theme. I define musical mainstream as follows: A reasonably stable body of music (call it "tradition") that exists at any given period of time in a relatively broad geographic area. We know quite obviously that, today, change is constant, that almost anything goes, but we are not always aware that our synagogue musical mainstream has undergone change—sometimes radical—throughout its long history going as far back as biblical times.[12]

New musical content—foreign and secular elements—has always entered the existent tradition. Change always took place, but what varied was the nature of change, which depended on just how the mainstream reacted to the intrusion of foreign elements. Reaction took place in two very opposite ways. First via a process called active assimilation, the other passive assimilation.

Active assimilation takes place when the old established tradition receives and absorbs the new elements to the extent that their original foreign character can hardly be detected. In this case the mainstream exerts its influence upon the new. It transforms the new—it Judaizes, Hebraizes, and makes religious the foreign material.

Passive assimilation, on the other hand, takes place when the existent musical entity permits the new to function, side by side, with the old—forcing no substantial change in its character. It simply attaches itself to the externals of the mainstream. In active assimilation, the mainstream dominates the new, in passive assimilation, the mainstream submits to the new. One should also be aware that these two opposites did not always function as extremes—there were times when compromise between the two took place.

Examples of passive assimilation are numerous, the more obvious phenomena taking place during critical periods of radical change in Jewish life: massive movements of migration and especially revolutionary movements.[13]

First, with the destruction of the Second Temple and emergence of the new synagogue, elements of Temple music were preserved, but dramatically new content needed to be established.

Set Two: Preservation and Innovation

This led to a number of Talmudic complaints as to the use of foreign tunes.[14] The Hasidim, for instance, accepted and even rationalized the use of Polish, Russian, and Slavic tunes.[15] The Reform movement—at least at first with its complete rejection of traditional mainstream—filled the musical vacuum with Protestant-like hymns.[16] Later, the liberal movement underwent moderate changes and returned some elements of the traditional mainstream.

At present, the collapse of prayer as a living experience, the confusion and ambiguity of God as a central force, the desire to preserve the institution of the synagogue and "worship" in spite of the above, and the penetration of Israel into the Diaspora culture all play a part the secularization of the synagogue. The mainstream has virtually disappeared. (Slight exception: We still have the need to preserve more vigorously many central elements of the High Holy Day service; the less frequent, the greater the desire to preserve.)

Lest we pass too hard judgment on the process of passive assimilation, we should keep in mind that most often, in the past especially, and even here and there today, when foreign elements were received without external change, they were assimilated experimentally—by the sheer energy of a living worship entity. The foreign was imbued with a believable sense of the sacred. The alien was transcended by spiritual purpose—by an intense and passionate relationship with God. Today we are doubly handicapped, both by the absence of any stable tradition, and by a weakening of transcending experiential energy.[17]

At this point it is proper to consider the question: Why did all of this happen? Did this intense and dynamic evolution of synagogue music have a purpose? What enabled or permitted such constant and often gross change to take place?

Change was possible because of the absence of institutional control. The institution of the rabbinate was able to control *halakhah* (Jewish Law), but not our music—totally and freely in the hands of the laity and cantor.

Up until the eighteenth century, there was virtually no notation—synagogue music was an oral tradition.[18] Radical change was stimulated by sudden geographic movements of large bodies of Jews, and their dramatic exposure to new musical idioms and styles. Most important, dynamic and free musical development was necessary to balance or to counter a static liturgy.

7. THE UNMOVABLE ANCHOR

Historians have labored hard to explain the remarkable phenomenon of the survival of the Jewish people. One of the most talked about theories stresses the fact that our people possessed an ingenious ability to sustain and reconcile two contradictory attitudes. One is to preserve and rigidly freeze, the other is to be openly flexible and adapt.[19]

The duality is best demonstrated when one looks at two particular static bodies of our tradition, and their dynamic counterparts. I am referring to the fixed written Torah and the *siddur* (prayer book), and their opposites, the free *midrashic* (investigative) literature and liturgical music. What is important about these countermovements is not only that one gave new life to the other, but that one contributed to the preservation—and perhaps even survival—of the other.

Torah is the unmovable anchor around which swim and play its creative embellishers: Midrash ("Exegesis") and music. But miraculously enough, without affecting one iota of change or deviation upon the anchor, the embellishments ensure its preservation.

You will pardon me if I use a *midrashic*-like analogy: A poor but resourceful wandering woman possesses but one garment of clothing, and the only way she can give some vitality to her dress (and to herself) is by embellishing it here and there—sometimes more superficially, sometimes more imaginatively. The garment *appears* to have been transformed. Yet in spite of the change, its fundamental entity is untampered, and so it survives both in substance and in spirit.

The Torah was zealously guarded against even the slightest change, and the *siddur* (prayer book), while at certain times did receive added material, did so under the strict unyielding proviso that, once entered, nothing may be removed, edited, or changed.[20]

For all of this stubborn rigidity, I think we ought to be thankful, for if the anchor itself should submit to change, slowly but surely it would be on the way to dissolution. But of course we must add our thanks to the freedom given to Midrash ("Exegesis") and especially to our synagogue music.

What has been the *nature* of change in our music is a larger subject to be touched upon. Suffice it to know that it has been ongoing from far back in biblical times until (and especially so) today. Our scribes of the past were uninterested in recording any description of musical content, but we have enough secondary comment that more than suggests change, especially when it led to excess.[21] There is evidence of a High Priest versus Levite conflict over the character of new music introduced in Second Temple worship, and later rabbinic concern over chanting certain Scripture with tavern melodies. There were also general concerns over the overindulgence of certain cantors borrowing music from the secular world, not to mention later blatant lifting of operatic material into the synagogue.[22]

There is one significant difference in the process of change between the past and present: In the past, change was slow and gradual, not sharply recognizable because of the strength and stability of the existent musical mainstream to absorb the new without being dominated by it.

Today, because new musical elements and oddities are slipping into our service, the mainstream has weakened—especially in the Reform movement—so that it has become helplessly passive. One ultimately pays the price for too much freedom.

Where am I in all of this? I feel blessed with the good fortune of having lived deeply in the two worlds I have addressed. Though I was a resistant youth who had to pray three times a day in a strict Orthodox yeshiva environment, I am honestly thankful for it. That deep-rootedness has enabled me to maintain a balance between two musical worlds: traditional and contemporary. I feel comfortable standing in the two worlds, and I can only hope that my music does in some way reflect this duality with gratification.

8. ASHKENAZI TRADITION

When we address the issue of music to text relationship, we should perhaps first raise the question as to whether the primary purpose of the musical content is to react to—to edify—the literalness of the text, or whether its function is to participate in the establishment of an atmosphere of *tefillah*—or both.

When we look at the immense repository of liturgical pieces that exists today, we can find many texts set to music of diverse and contradictory character—suggesting that the intent of the composer is to respond very often to needs other than the message of the word.[23]

For me, the key reason for this diversity lies in the static-dynamic relationship of liturgy and music. On the one hand we have a fixed and controlled prayer book unchanging in its central portions, joining with a highly active musical culture imbued with *laissez-faire* permissiveness. The more rigid one is, the freer the other.

While it is true that this static-dynamic relationship helps contribute to the ongoing vitality of *tefillah*, the persistent sameness of liturgy repeated in a strict and disciplined way tends to be so second nature that it becomes more of a pretext than a text for musical realization.[24]

Today, as fragmentation increases, so does diversity. The creative attitudes of composers toward the musical setting of the liturgy are immense and varied—insiders, outsiders, deep knowledge, superficial knowledge, partiality toward particular musical vocabulary.[25]

Every composer brings into his or her composition at least an unconscious element of bias. It is a rarity to find a composer who combines what we would consider all the positive ingredients—knowledge of language, intent to translate that knowledge musically into a piece that integrates itself into a larger stream of prayer—rather than to demonstrate skill, craft, or even originality.[26]

When we examine that remarkable system of *nusach* (traditional chant)—a phenomenon of an oral folk process—we witness as well the looseness and uncertainty—the gray area—regarding the link between music and text. As impressive as *nusach* is in its ability to control its various contents through an orally transmitted evolution, it has at the same time a built-in limitation with regard to its connection with the text. For the most part, *nusach* has a life and purpose of its own, and thus more often it directs the text and not the reverse.[27]

There are two reasons: First, the very stability of a particular *nusach* is imposed on a block of text in which the content of the parts often varies in character. As a result, we find that the need for a purely musical continuity transcends the needs of varying texts, which, if responded to, would lead to fragmentation.

Second, when we examine closely the actual character of the various melodies, we see that each of their distinct qualities—color, mood, texture—seem to have evolved out of conditions outside of the literal content of its particular liturgical passages.[28]

The *ma'ariv* (evening) service on *Rosh Hashanah* (New Year), for instance, as it functions more as a preliminary to the greater centrality of the holiday, tends to be cooler—less open to emotional expansion. Moreover, we also find the musical vocabulary designed with more distinct melodic qualities, which limit improvisational expansion.[29]

Shabbat, on the other hand, where one settles oneself more deeply in enjoying *tefillah* (prayer), we move from cool to warm to hot. Keep in mind that the Shabbat mode offers greater potential for emotional interpretation partially because its musical potential is drawn more out of real design and less out of motif derivation.[30] After all, *nusach* that has clear and distinct melodic motifs allows for less improvisational expansion.

I do not suggest that we abandon our link with the ideational content of the liturgy—even though we are aware of the congregational level of literacy.[31] It does, of course, have importance, but perhaps when we consider elevation we need to judge in terms of how it relates to the "religious" experience in *tefillah*.

The performer who knows Hebrew will dictate a contrasting musical character to bring the Hebrew text to life even though the music does not; he creates a relationship. On the other hand, if a performer who does not respond to the text sings music that does, he may destroy the relationship altogether.

9. ISRAEL'S INFLUENCE ON AMERICAN LIBERAL SYNAGOGUE MUSIC

When I first considered this topic, my thoughts turned initially toward an examination of the serious synagogue compositions of the past fifty years, and to investigate Israel's influence on the dynamic creative efforts of the American composer. How and to what extent has the musical culture of Israel entered the creative process—affecting the musical substance of our mainstream? Because this phase of our theme produced only a handful of musical works by composers who responded to Israel as isolated individuals rather than as part of a broader movement—and because of my increased awareness that the anticipated thrust and focus of our subject asked to be centered in the now—I subsequently turned my direction to the more immediate concern about Israel's relationship to American synagogue music today.

I wish not to minimize the worthiness of my original intent in spite of its relatively minor scope. I respect greatly the serious efforts of these few individual composers:

Lazare Saminsky (1882–1959), whose writing was often moved by his controversial concept, which leaps backward past the Diaspora into ancient Israel, as the only genuine source of Hebrew melodies.[32]

Jacob Weinberg (1879–1956), who based some of his compositions on Joseph's Yasser's (1893–1981) melodic and harmonic theory of the inherent pentatonic fundamental, which he saw as the authentic Hebraic element, again, linked to Israel of the past.[33]

Ernest Bloch (1880–1977), in a most abstract sense, was driven passionately by his deep connection with historical Israel and its prophetic impact when he produced the *Avodath Hakodesh* ("Sacred Service").[34]

And Abraham Wolf Binder (1895–1966) immersed himself in the musical folk character of 1950s Israel, and integrated it substantively into his writing in a creative and dynamic way.[35]

There are others as well, but perhaps another occasion will offer an opportunity to probe into this aspect of our theme. But now we turn to that area which has produced a great deal of heated polemic out of the turmoil of change now taking place in our synagogue lives.

My first response to the title "Israel's Influence on American Liberal Synagogue Music" was to see it as a question and not as a statement. Putting it into the form of a question demanded more serious attention to a clarification of what we mean precisely by these words. In probing the question I emerged with three prerequisite phenomena which, for me, demand examination: 1) What exactly are we speaking of when we use the term "influence"?; 2) What is the meaning of worship entity as a precondition to dynamic influence?; and 3) How does secularism act upon the religious experience and, more important, its reverse, how does the religious entity act upon the secular?

We will look into these three interrelated phenomena as they functioned both in our past synagogue history as well as in our present struggling process of change.

The idea of influence cannot be looked at merely as a simple cliché. It is in a deeper sense derived out of a sophisticated process. When an existing musical entity receives new elements into its body, it will react by either submitting passively to the new content, in form and style, without asserting itself—allowing for the new to function side by side with the old, unchanged in its character and original purpose—or it will direct its energies upon the new elements, shaping them, transforming them in a variety of ways so that they will, in the end, serve the existent mainstream. Influence here means a mutuality of purpose. In a word, the old *is* influenced by the new, but only by exerting its own influence on the new.[36]

Which of these two processes takes place will be determined by the strength, vitality, acceptance, and respect for the existing entity. The more the established entity is a living reality, the more it will act upon and influence the new. The more this entity loses its core force—its independence—the more it will submit itself to domination by the new.[37] I use the word domination because, in this case, influence does not actually take place.

What is this idea of a worship entity? To my mind, its central meaning lies in its independence. While it serves, at the same time it exists in and of itself—it has a life of its own. We who participate in it do not create it, per se, but rather enter into it, submit ourselves to its stream and substance. Its potential is not only that it is there, but more important, that we experience its presence and are able to submerge ourselves into its life. Though we may retain our individuality, the individual is subservient to the force and energy of the entity.

What actually constitutes entity is not always easily defined or recognized, for it is made up of both tangible and intangible forces in different states of balance, and in different situations. There are the obvious elements of form and continuity that for the most part are stable and predictable—a logical flow of liturgy to which a musical content responds with seriousness and respect. While these tangible elements are important, they alone cannot produce a worship entity without the presence of the intangible. Through my own life's experience, I have found the best words to describe this more elusive element of religious intent: the need and desire to enter a spiritual experience and to transcend the ordinary. God will be at the center of this religious intent for some; for others, God in man will suffice to motivate the act of elevation.[38]

The third area that needs to be examined before turning to our contemporary scene has to do with the secular. To begin with, the question as to what is secular and what is sacred, difficult as it is to answer, is not the prime issue pertinent to our theme. It is a fact of history that the secular has always been a major source out of which the synagogue—as well as the church—drew much of its raw material.[39] Indeed, one must not only acknowledge this but also see it as an integral condition within the entire process of the sacred experience. The sacred is not totally in itself an independent state or thing. It is the end result of the transformation of the ordinary state or thing into elevation. Because of this process, one might say that the sacred is actually in need of and perhaps even dependent upon the secular. Johann Sebastian Bach sharply demonstrated the validity of this process. One of the remarkable aspects of Bach was his conscious openness to a variety of new musical elements and styles that were developing during his time. He borrowed from the French dance to the opera, but it was his profound religious need that enabled him to actively assimilate and transform many of these secular ideas into the creation of some of his great sacred works.[40] So, what is essential here is not the content of the secular, per se, but rather the attitude imposed upon it.

The amazingly rich and varied tradition that has come to us from the past developed crucially out of the process of desecularization. With this in mind, let us look for a moment into the traditional synagogue of the past to see how the dynamics of influence functioned. The idea of passive and active assimilation is one of many concepts I have learned from my most respected teacher, Eric Werner.[41] It has often helped me understand the nature of synagogue musical development, and indeed serves this essay in a fundamental way in the concept of assimilation.

Active assimilation was a powerful process. The old absorbed the new to a point whereby the original character of the new might be virtually lost in transformation. Passive assimilation, on the other hand, received new musical content but allowed this content to retain its original shape and form. However, even though the old responded passively to the external new, assimilation nevertheless took place. The tune—or musical pattern— while it objectively retained its original external content, was transformed by the energy of a living worship entity in an experiential way. The force of religious intent penetrated the foreign elements of such musical material, submerging it into its own stream by imbuing it with serious and believable religious intent. The alien was transcended by spiritual purpose.

I bring out this past phenomenon to demonstrate what I consider the process of influence to be, so that with this in mind, we can raise the question not only of what Israel's influence on the music of today's synagogue has been, but whether or not there has been in fact any influence at all keeping in mind that we are considering the question of influence upon our music and not on synagogue worship per se.

Over the past several years, a body of song material has been taken into the American synagogue from Israel, a substantial part of which is drawn from the so-called Hasidic festival phenomenon.[42] Both the eagerness with which we have seized upon these songs and the manner in which we have used them need to be seen as part of a growing and unconscious fundamental change in the direction of worship. At the heart of this change is the slide into secularization. I see it happening not because we consciously wish to secularize our worship experience, but because we are more and more caught up in the breakdown of a worship entity and the weakening of its prime mover: religious and spiritual intent. The secular always contributes to the sacred, but when the sacred diminishes, the secular is not only allowed to retain its own character, but also participates in the further weakening of spiritual energies.[43] As the need and ability for transcendence over the ordinary decreases, so does the secular exert its domination. These songs, therefore, have not influenced the mainstream of synagogue music in the dynamic sense because our weakening religious potential has stood by passively, incapable of asserting its influence over the secular elements of many of these songs.

And so we use them as an end in themselves. How do we use them? To begin with, we lose a sense of discrimination in how we select these songs. While it is not in the purpose of this paper to analyze these tunes, nevertheless we have to acknowledge a certain degree of character differences amongst these materials. There are some tunes that approach the genuineness of the folk as well as the classical Hasidic quality (e.g., *Y'did Nefesh*—"Beloved of My Soul"). There are some that merely attempt to achieve this but end up as a mixture of the contrived and the pop. And finally there are those tunes that are permeated with the pop—totally commercial in character (e.g., *Bashanah*—"In the Year").

Selectivity, as I see it, means the desire to search out that which can be assimilated into religious experience. Some tunes more easily achieve this because they contain basic elements that emerge out of established sacred substance, and in themselves can evoke the spiritual spark—if we would but recognize this substance. I say this particularly because we have been exposed through Israeli recordings to some of these tunes, presented in both style and arrangement that belong in the cabaret and not in the synagogue.[44] Such popularization blinds the listener to the presence of core quality and the potential seriousness of the tune. The danger here is the carrying over into the synagogue the commercial façade of the tune and not its inherent religious value.

There are, of course, those tunes that virtually defy any attempt to relate them to the sacred. The catchiness of such tunes is to be looked at with caution for it is very often this element that reveals its popular intent— resisting all efforts toward transformation thereby serving only immediate needs of stimulus.[45]

Immediacy of needs touches off its opposite: the sustaining possibility of these melodies. I have often marveled at how some of the old synagogue tunes, not extraordinary in their character, have been able to sustain themselves for long periods of time. Part of the answer must lie in the fact that they have not been experienced as independent tunes as such. They have been so integrated into the total worship entity so that the critical aspect of their content becomes irrelevant. I never tire of the old *Etz Chayim* ("Tree of Life") melody because it serves that least shakable entity of the Torah service. The state of reverence that still pervades this part of the service permits this simple, classically pure melody to sustain itself on and on. On the other hand, how often have we become frustrated when we realized how eagerly we received such tunes as Nurit Hirsch's *Oseh Shalom* ("Maker of Peace"), only to find ourselves tiring of it in relatively short time.[46]

Another area in which some of these tunes contribute to the diffusion of the entity is where we use them in the context of the service. This same *Oseh Shalom*, with all of its limitations, might function more naturally at the close of the service. But when it is now often substituted for the "May the Words" at the end of the *Amidah* ("Standing Prayer"), when quiet meditation is the mood of the moment, then we see demonstrated total disregard for the entity. Respect for the stable continuity of the service begs for sensitivity of the context.

Perhaps most crucial is the manner in which these melodies are presented. Tempo is often a critical element. Many of these festival tunes have a spiritual possibility only when sung in more moderate tempi. Here lies one of the greatest misconceptions with regard to the classical Hasidic *niggun* (wordless melody).[47] A *niggun* was never rushed. Space in time was understood as a prerequisite for entrance into the energy of the tune. The *niggun* sung in the lighthearted state of haste reflects the singers' shallow, sometimes frivolous grasp of the tune. What more can one say about the manner of singing? Which direction shall one take the tune—out into the streets, or up into the higher places? Does the externality of the tune dominate the singer, or does the singer control the loftier essence of the tune? Where there is no religious intent, it is the ordinary we bring into the synagogue—which ultimately brings the synagogue down to the ordinary.

This growing submission to secularization has struck me not only in how it has affected our attitude toward the new, but equally so with regard to the old—and by this I mean in particular the musical mainstream of the liberal synagogue—developed during the past one hundred years or so. I think it has begun to take its toll. We are dealing with a vicious cycle. The more the character of the pedestrian permeates the service, the less are we, as well as our congregations, able or willing to receive and respond to the more serious and potentially inspirational music of our past. A clear symptom of this process is the slow but gradual diminishing of choir participation, whereby a rich and valuable segment out of our creative past is being left by the wayside. This vicious cycle subtly influences the way we as cantors, as well as rabbis and music directors, relate to the essence of this literature. Secularization begins to dull our very own perception of the inherent inspirational value of much of this literature.[48] We begin to see this music at worst as cerebral—intellectual—or at best as merely aesthetic. The waning drive to ascend clouds the soul level of much of this music, causing us not only to shy away from it but, even when we perform it, we often do so without inner conviction—with an unconscious sense of apology, leaving only the externals to come forth. The spark of holiness is present somewhere—seeking it out requires a persistent religious will, particularly in the face of the growing impact of the secular.

I can speak of this out of my own experience. In the past several years I have found myself avoiding some of this literature. I have now begun to revive some of those works—but I do so with great deliberation, insisting that we sing only that music in which we have been able to discover—and hopefully realize—the spiritual essence inherent in it. When this does take place, then my belief in the validation of such serious music today is once again reinforced. This holds true for our tradition of *nusach* (traditional chant) and *hazzanut* (cantorial art).

Finally, returning to the core question of our theme, and in the light of my understanding of it, it is perhaps needless to say that influence, in the deepest sense, has not as yet taken place. The reality of Israel's presence and its secular thrust may very well have cut into American synagogue life, reinforcing its gravitation toward the secular, but to see Israel as having specifically influenced our music cannot be considered in the critical sense. Perhaps such influence has yet to come. As we realize the inevitable transience of many of the Hasidic festival tunes, we will either reject them or, hopefully, be moved to act upon them out of newly discovered religious energy. There are, perhaps, some beginnings amongst some of our creative forces. Time and history will ultimately answer the question: Shall synagogue music once again assert itself, or shall it submit itself?

7

Set Three: Sacred and Secular

10. THE BORN BELIEVER

Very few people approach prayer at unfixed times when there may be an unexpected need to address a deity—when not bound to a liturgical structure or to a place. They are not spontaneously directed, but respond to a complex of outer entities. In the face of all of this, should we not be moved to consider that, without environmental support and direction, true prayer might live a precarious existence? By this, I mean to confront the hard question: whether belief, prayer and deity can exist without a learning process.

I am reminded of an experience Franz Rosenzweig had when he first came into contact with an Eastern European Jewish community. Commenting on the absolute totality of Eastern European Jewish identity, he said: "Here the five year olds already live in a context of three thousand years."[1]

I recall this when I look upon the true believer, who simply cannot imagine another existence because he was almost literally born in a state of belief. He lives in the context of three thousand years. His power of belief is so deep because his learning process existed without utter awareness of learning.

11. THE SEEKING OF GOD AND KNOWLEDGE OF GOD'S EXISTENCE

Does the seeker of God do so out of a knowledge that God exists? Or does the seeker, although he has never "met" God, nevertheless do so out of secondhand knowledge—that is, having been influenced by the believing culture?

The seeker, witnessing the elevated state of the believer, often wishes to avoid the primary and difficult prerequisite of a deity, having instead the intent to seek the achievement of "transcendence." After all, if the seeker has never experienced God, how will he know the validity of an assumed discovery?[2]

Along with the nonbelievers who utilize prayer for secondary purposes—secular, ethnic, or communal needs—one must consider seriously those who also lack belief inwardly, but who are aware somehow that the experience of belief can be useful, as the "acting out" of prayer may lead to an elevated, transcendent state.

How then does one become a "true believer"? Does one seek out the sacred, discover it, and become awestruck by the mysteries of it all? Does one at some point or another in life reach a particular moment of "eureka"? Can one become a "true believer" without the influence of another—isolated from an environment of believers?[3]

When one is brought up in an environment where total belief is the very air one breathes, the experience of belief is *the* way of life. Should one not consider this achievement a result of a training process? What happens when one is separated from a pure childlike unquestioning belief— a belief that one had no need to discover because it was already there?

Once one leaves this condition or even steps out of it for a moment to look at it—or, God forbid, to question it—then there is no way to come home again; no way to return to its core—to be totally captured by it.

If one prays to God not out of a deep and spontaneous need to be "in touch" with God, but rather out of the hidden agenda—that is, its usefulness for self-betterment—then such self-conscious prayer will achieve little.[4] The very knowledge that it is useful already condemns the act to inefficacy.

We may long for prayer in a nostalgic way, or we may want it again because we recognize in it potential values—morality, self-realization, historical memory, cultural enrichment—as an ally in our quest for transcendence.

All of these beliefs have in one way or another a link with extraneous agendas, and cannot be realized in the deepest sense.

Tied to a function, many do not believe prayer is essential to Judaism in the most natural sense, as breathing is to living.[5]

As a result, prayer and the Torah continue to touch our lives far less for their moral conceptions—teachings—but because they link us with a mystic illusion of the past. There are so few mysteries that penetrate our innermost selves. We preserve the charisma of the Torah by enclosing it in the holy ark, *davening* (praying) it, parading it about with reverence, but do we take it into our minds and action?

We tend to subtly express apologies along with pride as we navigate the high principles of the Torah, but do we take its contents into our own lives?

12. THE "SECULAR SIDE" OF THE JEW

In its literalness, the prayer book and its content serve religious needs connected with a God relationship; yet at the same time, it functions as a kind of internal piece of literature that reinforces an ethnic identification—the "secular side" of the Jew.[6] What is to be observed from this is that when the religious stream of prayer is actively engaged, stability prevails and change in worship is minimal or unnoticeably gradual. And when the religious factor is weakened, quicker change is seen in the musical content.

Today in the liberal movements, where the preservation of Jewish identity is largely motivated by secular needs, there is still a desire to reconcile the secular in the cloak of the sacred, and we are scrambling around to deal with the contradiction—to make it work.[7] We are compelled to keep the place of our tradition, but do not know what to do with it. Are we then simply "acting out" all of the elements that make up the phenomenon of worship? Is this amateur-like effort not part of the fear of a losing struggle to preserve the institution itself?

From our earliest period as a Diaspora society—from the Babylonian exile until this very day—the greatest motivating force for our existence has been that remarkable passion to survive as a separate people.[8] Underlying this stubbornness for survival was a foundation of *separateness*. We are and will always be distinguished from all the peoples of the world.

Still, the Jewish people have had to struggle with the tension between preserving our tradition and facing the influence of foreign cultures in which we have lived. This tension can be observed in a most active way in the history of synagogue music.

While the sacred written words succeeded valiantly against foreign influence, our musical tradition was much more open to foreign intrusion and, as a result, to change—though how much change and how fast the pace of the change varied. When the tradition was strong and stable, and when it did receive foreign musical elements, the tradition was able to absorb, digest, and dominate these new elements—so much so that they would no longer be recognizable. They were swallowed up by the tradition—change was slow.

On the other hand, when the musical tradition weakened, the foreign would dominate. There was no foundation from which to firmly defend our musical tradition. This latter phenomenon has unfortunately become the dominant trend today, as Judaism collides with modernity.[9]

Unlike today, in the distant past virtually all *hazzanim* (cantors) emerged out of a singular meticulous mainstream—a mainstream that was secure in itself and its influences.[10] There were obvious differences in talent and voice, yet they were all rooted in a singular synagogue culture from childhood to apprenticeship to *bima* (pulpit), with no preoccupation with problems and solutions.

Today, however, more and more *hazzanim* enter the synagogue with this preoccupation, a reality further complicated by the many paths and intentions they take to the synagogue—their own synagogue history (or lack thereof); their cultural background; divergent musical backgrounds; varying Hebrew literacy—all of which feed into personal biases, strengths, and weaknesses. As an aside, this is why, unlike the synagogues of the past, today each synagogue evolves its own personality.[11] This, in itself, represents a worship problem.

Surely, the very quest for a worship solution has a built-in no-win dilemma—the very idea of solving the problem of prayer is self-contradictory. Most worship "experiments"—with pop music, English text, and the like—fail because we are asking secular devices to lift us into the realm of the sacred when the devices have themselves remained untransformed.

13. SACRED MUSIC AS "CULTURE"

I was sitting in a synagogue on a Sunday evening about to hear a concert of contemporary Jewish music—liturgical for the most part—when suddenly *déja vu*! There I was some forty years ago sitting in a large Orthodox *shul* (synagogue) on a Sunday evening listening to what was then known as a *ma'ariv* (evening) concert. Some of the greats were still around showing their *schtiklach* (gimmicks)—usually major compositions that were unusable during the regular Shabbat or Yom Tov (holiday) services.

What sparked the déja vu? Was it simply the coincidence of a weekday liturgical concert? Or did I sense a more significant connection between the two rather dissimilar environments?

Soon came the realization that what happened then in the Orthodox *shul* (synagogue) and what is happening now in the liberal synagogue are both part of the very same process. A process that says: When sacred music loses its connection to the sacred experience, it becomes "culture." That is, when such music no longer functions as a stimulus to prayer, it leaves the synagogue of worship to become an historical matter, a culture to be preserved.[12] How does this happen?

Religious music—be it the *hazzanut* (cantorial art) or the creative liturgical compositions of the liberal synagogue—developed initially out of immediate experiential needs within worship. It came to heighten a clearly defined entity of prayer and, when it was at its best, it integrated itself into the spiritual whole.[13]

Hazzanut, in its loftiest periods, was not separated from the totality of prayer—that is, now we *daven*, now the *hazzan* sings. *Hazzanut* was a natural extension of *davening*. It was a passionate artistic response to the religious energy emanating from the deep spontaneous *davening* of the congregation.[14] In this context, even the act of listening became integrated into the larger spiritual experience. Listening did not interrupt the sacred.

But when the passion and pathos of prayer began to lose its religious fervor, and the spirit of synagogue worship turned toward communal-ethnic identity needs, the very substance of *davening*, *hazzanut* and the listening experience all took on radical changes. *Davening* became a style, a surface cultural expression or at its worst an "acting out." *Hazzanut* became something of the past to preserve but lacking the fire. The *hazzan* became an object of nostalgia and a functional clergyman who self-consciously faces the congregation. And, finally, listening became relegated to another separate element in a series of "prayer activities."

As a consequence, *hazzanut* declined, and when any art declines there rises up a need to preserve. The recording industry took over, the concert phenomenon developed, the secular *mavin* (expert) no longer had to go to synagogue on Shabbat: he could now listen to records, turn on the radio, or go to a *ma'ariv* concert. *Hazzanut* lost its religious purpose and became "culture."[15]

Oddly enough, this very same process has been taking place in the liberal synagogue over the last few decades. During the 1930s and '40s, a major renaissance of serious musical creativity arose in the Reform movement.[16] This burst of creativity responded to an evolving worship character that asked for greater musical aesthetic and sophistication. Though the involvement of the congregant may have been cooler and more passive, there was a serious atmosphere of prayer—a stream of spirituality, introspective though it may have been. "Listening" to music of a more aesthetic quality flowed naturally out of a larger sense of sacredness. It did not interrupt the stream of prayerfulness.

As we move toward our times, when more and more the institution of worship is becoming an external façade for more secular needs, and the sense of sacred gives way to communal involvement, sacred music becomes an anomaly. Professional choirs give way, ultimately, to congregational singing—to the point where the vast library of serious synagogue music sits on the shelf during most of the year except for one or two occasions when a handful of pieces are dusted off to be presented in concert. Sacred music of the past is now added to a list of religious elements that are exhibited from time to time for historical purposes. On some occasions new "sacred" works have been created with the special event in mind rather than the week-to-week synagogue needs.[17]

Sitting in the synagogue that Sunday evening triggered two additional recollections that said it all. The first, more recent, was of a conversation with a talented and dedicated cantorial graduate of a school of sacred music. He had studied and mastered, seriously, a vast literature of synagogue composition—from the classics to the contemporary—but now sadly finds little use for it during most of the year.

The second came years back when a premier Orthodox *hazzan* sadly informed me of his departure from the *bima* (pulpit) to sell insurance. The turning point took place the day the *rav*—or rabbi—began to announce the pages. His decision was sealed when one of his regular *shul*-goers asked him after a fulfilling Shabbat *davening*, *"Chazen, vos zingt ihr azoy fil?"* (Chazzan, why are you singing so much?)

14. IN SEARCH OF RELEVANCE

It should be clear to most people that the institution of worship is in an ambiguous and problematic state—not knowing for sure where to go and, at the same time, determined to somehow preserve itself.

We have looked for answers in every conceivable corner of the worship complex—from liturgy to language to change in the music. Volunteer choir and no choir; cantor and song leader; congregational singing and traditional chant; old tunes and new tunes; Israeli tunes and camp tunes—underlying all these is the desire to engage the congregation so as to bring relevance to the tradition, and to justify its preservation. Here and there we have felt occasional gratification, although we were not always certain it was the actual substance of change and not the stimulus of change itself that affected us. In any event, real, ongoing and sustaining value was hard to find. And so we continue to search for ways—not wanting to let go—groping for a fragment of relevance in the institution.

Are we looking for new relevance when the thing itself is perhaps no longer meant to be? Are we trying to keep alive a phenomenon that was meant to be one thing by trying to form it into something else because we have nothing in sight to replace it with, to serve certain needs? It is at this point that one has to turn to an inner-view.

Throughout our history, the character of worship—style, music, and choreography—was shaped by the particular relationship of the secular and the sacred.[18] Defining the sacred element in absolute terms is no easy task, but in broad terms, sacred refers to that which is motivated by a deep sense of religiosity, usually in relationship with God or the divine, and often expressed through the dynamics of prayer.[19] The experience produced can be described as transcending the ordinary, entering a state of awe or spirituality, where some level of sophistication is at play.

On the other hand, the secular can be described as the ordinary, everyday experience where communal involvement and reinforcement is motivated by that persistent need to preserve our ethnic link and identity to the people of Israel.[20]

The phenomenon of synagogue worship always fulfilled its function when the sacred component was actively present and sustained over an extended period of time. During the longest period of the Diaspora leading up to the Enlightenment, the sacred—though totally integrated into the secular and vice versa—was ever-present as the primary motivation for prayer.[21]

With the Enlightenment and rise of the liberal movement in the eighteenth and nineteenth centuries, the idea of Judaism as a religion dominated the entity of worship, while the secular-ethnic-peoplehood side diminished to relative insignificance. What is important is that what shaped the notion of a service and motivated its experience was a need to reach out for the sacred.[22]

There is no question that the prayer book in the life of the worshiping Jew acted as an identity preserver, and was vital to the powerful bond with the people of Israel. But what sustained its validity and stability was its religious foundation and relationship with the sacred. As long as the secular and the sacred were in some reasonable balance, stability prevailed as worship actually integrated itself into the way of life of the Jew. When certain processes enter into the natural unself-conscious behavior of people, what can be immediately observed is the absence of ongoing change. Change in worship during these stable periods was minimal, or so gradual that one was unaware of it.

15. WHAT KIND OF MUSIC IS CONDUCIVE TO WORSHIP?

When I think about this question, I hesitate very seriously because, to put it bluntly, I feel that only God knows for sure what the answers are. It would be humanly impossible, indeed presumptuous, of me or of any individual to objectively formulate specific definitions for a music that is conducive to the various forms of worship—all the more so to try to break down such music into its many ingredients: melody, harmony, rhythm, text, etc.

We have never been blessed with prophets of synagogue music. Throughout the history of synagogue music, and even during its more stable periods, arbitrariness was always present in various degrees. But arbitrariness in the past was more often dominated or controlled by the dependable anchor of the mainstream. Today the extreme reverse has taken place. The mainstream that once existed has submitted itself almost totally to arbitrariness—to the point where the mainstream has either become so weak that it is powerless or has perhaps even disappeared.[23]

This in itself explains the preoccupation of our subject matter with a host of external specifics and details, losing sight of the larger concern: *essence*. Essence and mainstream are as interdependent as body and soul—without essence the mainstream will flounder and dissipate.

In more detail, the pattern that has grown in recent years can be seen as a radical shift in emphasis between two antagonistic poles: a shift from the ideal to the reality; from the theatrical to the practical; from the concern with the long range to a concern with immediacy; from a desire for a sustained yet dynamic mainstream to a fragmented, constantly changing body of musical stimuli; and to quote Dr. Einstein's excellent phrase: "From conscious and sensitive accommodation to accidental accommodation— accommodation for its own sake."

But beneath all of these shifts in focus resides one central fundamental of change: the movement from the sacred to the secular and its primary movers—transcendence to the ordinary.

I lay these observations out before you for serious consideration and confrontation, because without them it would be a futile task to attempt to answer the specific question in our subject title. Indeed, there would be far less need to even deal with the specifics. As long as our "worship" continues its submission to the secular and the ordinary—as long as we relate to the service superficially—it would be pointless to formulate guidelines as to what kind of music is conducive for worship. Concern with melody, harmony, rhythm, etc., constitutes the cart before the horse, for it is misleading logic to suppose that it is the penetration of a musical conglomeration and chaos into the synagogue that has produced secularization. I see the reverse as true. It is our very loss of touch with the sacred, the transcendent, the essence that has opened the doors for the secular, the ordinary, the anything.[24]

The sacred, a term that we have come to use glibly, when it is alive in one's heart and soul has a power all its own to direct one to the specifics within worship. It insists on more sensitive selectivity, discretion, and equality; it produces energies that can transform, elevate, and spiritualize a musical content that hovers about the secular—or, is sometimes even downright secular. The term "sacred" has become a label. The heart, magic, and mystery of the word have faded. Because we have become, often unwillingly, conditioned—even dominated—by the secular, we have become, unknowingly, desensitized to the sacred. As a result, many of us seriously and frustratingly struggle with a higher notion of *tefillah* (prayer) when, to begin with, we are already under the influence and power of the secular. It is ultimately a losing battle. The secular has entered the framework of the sacred and is dominating it.

8

Set Four: Past and Future

16. *L'DOR V'DOR*: FROM GENERATION TO GENERATION

When my Orthodox father first heard I had entered the Reform movement professionally as a *hazzan* (cantor), his response was silence. It became clear to me that he could be neither critical nor supportive of my decision. He controlled his troubled heart at my move into a virtually foreign religion—what he saw as the epitome of the *chukat hagoy* (manner of the Gentiles). He repressed any expression he might have felt.

He concealed his displeasure because I was a devoted son with whom a rift would surely disrupt his need for peace within the home. Peace was to be preserved at almost any cost—barring intermarriage.

Nevertheless, I was very comfortable joining him in *his* environment during my yearly visits to New York. I would sometimes spend an entire Shabbat with him—going to *shul* (synagogue), sharing Shabbat meals and, of course, a nap and a stroll. He even showed a touch of pride, albeit in a guarded way, when he introduced me to his acquaintances. My professional vocation was never mentioned; he would just say, "Meet my son from Los Angeles."

It was meaningful enough for him to simply show me as a son at home in his world. After all, I could take on *davening* in his *shul*, and I could put on a good show with "small talk"—Yiddish conversation.

There were occasions when I would arrive at his apartment when Shabbat was already in progress. Though I knew he would rather have it otherwise, he would avoid any negative comment, especially since he knew that I would be discreet in parking my car at a very safe distance to avoid embarrassment.

17. FUTURE MODELS OF WORSHIP

In struggling with my response to the subject at hand, I find myself thinking in two directions. One is that of uncertainty about what is to be in the future, the other of a certainty of that which needs to be now. Knowing only what can be achieved and experienced with some fulfillment today will be the start of a process that will determine what is to be in the future (unknown as it may be).

And so, I find it quite difficult to think productively of our theme: models for the future. The unknown of the years to come is overwhelming, and to try to leap into this unknown while still in the present state of groping may be skirting the primary focus. Indeed, such a future-oriented search can easily become an accessible diversion away from the frustrations of today.

With this in mind, I approach such questions as authenticity of liturgy for future days with much hesitation. I find it impossible to formulate, no less concretize, that which is to be authentic for the future.

I do not believe that authenticity can be isolated as an objective entity divorced from a complex of conditions that in actuality brings about its realization. What makes something authentic is much more than the very process of its becoming and much less its consciously preconceived model. Authenticity is the *by-product* of a long development of discovering, digesting, performing, and assimilating, and not a fixed, idealized beginning.[1]

This is not to say that in searching to fulfill one's needs today, we ignore the authenticity of the past. We do need this rich reservoir of literature, but we might draw from it with a freedom and spontaneity that we feel moved to experience today and not necessarily that which was authentic for the past.[2]

Reverence for the authentic of the past can appear as a worthy and lofty concept, but it can too easily transform us into preservers and caretakers. To preserve is noble, but to do so without entering and experiencing that which we preserve will only satisfy the pride of the collector.

And so I turn now to that other direction of certainty—that which I can speak of with some sense of reality. It has to do with preparation, although I think I would prefer to use the word "building."

Preparation suggests a narrow and immediate intimacy. How can we prepare for this Shabbat—and again next Friday night—and on, and on? We search for ways to stimulate involvement, very little growing out of these disconnected efforts.

A building process, however, which has no immediate expectation of gratification, is so much more difficult to take on, because it asks one to enter an act in trust—to repeat and build on it without knowing clearly and precisely what its ultimate will be.[3] Experience of deeper value can rarely come without an expanding foundation.

That which specifically needs such a building process is the Hebrew language and its musical extension. These elements still offer the highest potential for binding Jews together, for liberating them as individuals and for elevating them out of the ordinary of worship.[4] I do not think we will ever leave our present state of flitting from one stimulant to anther as long as the Hebrew language remains a superficial external in our synagogue lives.

I have participated in many worship situations, and I could almost always measure the depth of involvement in the congregation by the level of literacy with the Hebrew language. I feel that we have not approached its study seriously because it does not come instantly, because it demands a trusting commitment to a sustaining process of building, because we may even fear it as an unreachable magic or mystery. We today are incapable of experiencing with depth prayer in the English language.[5] At best, we read our English liturgy while our *inner* selves are not in touch with its words. Words read or sung in Hebrew out of an expanding knowledge of the language penetrate our Jewish psyche and expand the *substance* of our identity, remaining with us—always present for ongoing experiences. With the Hebrew language internalized, we would have less need for constant external stimulants.

The English language will always be necessary, but its use would be limited to a reflection on the changing day-to-day, or year-to-year, concerns. Transliteration of Hebrew is a superficial answer to our needs. It is a crutch and only perpetuates separation from the core of our culture. If one cannot read Hebrew, it would be far better to memorize a text or song.[6]

Language enrichment makes possible the broadening and deepening of the musical content of the service. As long as we are culturally and linguistically marginal, we will tend to cling to a limited body of music; a handful of liturgical tunes that represent for many the only fragile link to the stream.

The development of a more deeply enriching musical content also demands the patience and discipline through time. Today we are often prone to seize upon melodies that are achievable instantly, ignoring others that have greater depth and sustaining value, because they demand more time to explore.

There are few things in the life of the soul that can come into being without the discipline of repetition and patience and trust.

18. CAN YOU ACHIEVE PRIVACY IN PUBLIC?

Many Jewish congregants feel a heightened inner feeling when the rabbi or cantor faces the Ark—one seeking prayer, the other chanting. Several of our congregants have told me of such an awareness at this time during the service.

Why should this happen? One might quickly explain that the confrontation with the open ark can in itself stimulate a dramatic involvement.[7] While this may be true, I nevertheless suspect that there is more to it.

First, I wonder whether the congregant at this particular time may not be achieving a greater sense of freedom in that he is entering a state of privacy. He cannot see the faces of those on the pulpit and, more important, he cannot be seen. He can now be alone. He is free to feel. There is nothing between him and, well, anything he may wish to meet.[8]

A suggestion of this, curiously enough, can take place in the concert hall, for there are some listeners who are more open to instrumental performers than they are to singers. The instrumentalist may be seen as one immersed in a relationship with an instrument, who usually does not even face the audience directly. He can more easily surround himself with a cloak of privacy. The singer, though, faces his audience directly and focuses his performance immediately to them. Here there is a much greater struggle with self-consciousness; there can be no illusion of aloneness. Awareness of performance by both the singer and the audience cannot easily be brushed aside.

This intrusive element of performance takes us back to the sanctuary with the rabbi and cantor facing the Ark, when they appear to be more immersed in their own experience, after turning away from the congregation, with little or no self-consciousness of performance. With everyone now facing the same way, all can now experience a sense of equality and freedom. This sensing of equality may also suggest believability—that is, he is praying, not to me or for me. He himself is praying. He is really doing that which he wishes I could do. I believe him.[9]

Such a concept of equality and privacy was at one time a crucial part of worship, when the cantor chanted the entire service with his back to the congregation. It was only with the rise of the Reform movement, when both he and the rabbi turned to the congregation (reversing their roles as well), that the character of worship changed fundamentally. Where once they were participants, now they became officiants.

The music of the service responded to the change as well. Out of a spontaneous and primitive-like improvised style of chant came a formal, restrained and sometimes inflexible expression.[10]

The art of cantorial improvisation in the Reform movement is virtually gone. The art of improvisation could thrive only in the atmosphere of the old pulpit, where the presence of inner equality could free imagination, which is of course the basis for improvisation. Today's pulpit makes such spontaneity difficult to achieve. The only hope may lie in the ability of rabbi, cantor, and congregation to cultivate the art of privacy without anyone turning around.

19. THE AMERICAN SYNAGOGUE IN SEARCH OF ITS MUSICAL IDIOM

In response to the theme at hand, I consider it important that we first look into the idea of "search" and some of its implications. What interests me, primarily, is the particular framework that motivates and directs the process of search today.

To begin with, I believe that a clear concept of what we are searching for does not exist, as yet, for we are at present witnessing only the very beginning of a period of transition. Instability is the dominant character of today's worship. We have broken with the stable entity of the past and are now struggling for a substitute without any clear and convincing knowledge of what is to be. As difficult and frustrating as this may be for many of us, this is the very nature of our present historical reality.

It is needless to say that underlying our groping for a new and meaningful musical idiom is the struggle to discover a new concept of worship itself.[11] The character of synagogue music, if it is to reach a defined realization, will take place only after the idea of worship itself finds its purpose. In the absence of a defined goal, the idea of search becomes, at best, exploration and experimentation, and at its worst, a groping to fill an empty vacuum.

In the meantime, how can we seriously commit ourselves to the process of search even in the face of the unsettling state in which we find ourselves? I see today's activity of search as being directed by three distinct needs: (1) The needs of today's congregations; (2) The needs of the individual functionaries—cantor, composer, and choir director; (3) The need to preserve the continuity with the musical culture of the past.

These three motivations are presently active in our synagogues today in various degrees of stress—in various states of balance. While they cannot exist in the same state of balance, uniformly, in all of our synagogues, I consider them all as essential guidelines. They are to be respected with some reasonable equality; to totally ignore any one of these three needs or to exaggerate any one of them is harmful to the institution of worship. Yet all of these also invite potential danger, perhaps even contributing to future problems that may be difficult to undo.

Among these three needs, the need to preserve the continuity with our past musical culture—which includes our serious writings (art music) as well as the tradition of *nusach* (traditional chant) and *hazzanut* (cantorial art)—is of paramount importance. I stress this need for three reasons: (1) We have a moral historical obligation to preserve in substantive measure the music of the past; (2) Much of the music of the past still retains its potential to beautify worship and move the worshiper; (3) Even if there were a totally convincing rationale that our past literature is no longer relevant today, it would be difficult to reverse such a rationale should the time come when this stage may pass, and the synagogue may once again find itself in need of such music.[12]

It would be an awesome responsibility, indeed presumptuous, to break sharply with the past, for who can be so wise as to know what our needs may be even in the near future? However, to shape worship music totally within the framework of the past is to live wishfully in an ivory tower. For this reason, preservation of the traditions of the past must be weighed carefully with the needs of today's congregations and its functionaries. To be a meaningful and living enterprise, synagogue music must be simultaneously linked to our rich heritage and relevant to the needs of today.

20. WHY CAN'T A WOMAN CHANT LIKE A MAN?*

The movement for equal rights has steadily made its way onto the synagogue pulpit. The Reform movement has already removed all distinctions, with women rabbis and cantors increasing in number. The Conservative wing is not too far behind, although the gap between de jure and de facto recognition can be expected to remain for a while. Mainstream Orthodoxy prefers to ignore the matter altogether except that it is now beginning to react to some rumblings on the part of small but vocal neo-Orthodox

---

*This essay was written in 1985. The Reform movement began investing women cantors in 1975, and the Conservative movement instituted the practice in 1987. The inclusion of women in the cantorate has continued to generate controversy, as well as important musical changes, in the synagogue.

groups who are about to challenge the very foundation of a male entity of worship, and consequently the very sanctity of *halakhah* (Jewish Law) itself.[13]

Though discussion of women cantors in particular focuses primarily on the two issues of *halakhah* and *minhag* (custom), one should also keep in mind a third, less argued, ingredient: the very character of *hazzanut* itself.

With regard to *halakhah*, serious and rational debate usually ends up as a futile exercise. After all, *halakhah* is not an independent objective entity; it is fraught with subjective selectivity because its interpretation is ultimately bound up with practice. One interprets *halakhah* either to support the preservation of a particular practice or to officially accept a change in a practice that has, in fact, already become widespread—a way of life.[14] I might add that sometimes its purpose is in fact to preserve itself.

If one searches rabbinic sources vigorously enough and interprets outrageously enough, one could find support for just about any side of the issue. Meg. 23a, for instance, states, our rabbis taught that all are qualified to be among the seven (called up to read the Torah) even a woman or a minor, but the sages said that a woman should not read the Torah out of respect for the congregation (*k'vod hatzibbur*—i.e., "what it is accustomed to"). Cultural conditioning, the prime mover of *halakhah*, ultimately determines the status of practice. When and how a practice changes depends on the depth of conditioning within one's own ethnic-religious experience, as well as the extent of the outer cultural influence.

Within Orthodoxy, a female cantor is utterly out of the question. A woman *sheliach tzibbur* (messenger of the congregation) would represent a foreign, almost *goyish*-like intrusion into the well-guarded sanctity of a male Jewish worship culture. In a recent Orthodox-rabbinic deliberation on the issue, the principle of *chukat hagoy* was invoked: the practice that in any way reflects the manner of the gentile (Christian) is invalid.[15] In reality, however, any discussion within Orthodoxy on women cantors would be totally irrelevant as long as the practice of *mechitzah* (separation of men and women) remains intact.

Within the Conservative movement, official acceptance of women cantors is surely around the corner—following closely behind the recognition of women rabbis.[16] But one should not expect widespread de facto acceptance of equality for a while. Unlike the Reform service, the Conservative mode of *tefillah*, for the most part, continues to be conducted by the *hazzan*. The deep association with the old Orthodox tradition along with the continued presence of enough "old time" *daveners* will slow down the process. But when the Conservative service becomes more and more Reform-like in character and style—the rabbi conducting the order of the service, more English reading, the *hazzan* functioning more and more as a "soloist"—and when the next generation remembers less and less of the past, then will the doors of the Conservative service open wider to women cantors. The fact that there are already women singing on Conservative pulpits is, I suspect, due less to streaks of liberalness than to other factors: a decreasing interest and availability of male candidates, that positions open to women are usually part-time, making them attractive to the growing needs of women in exploration of new professions, as well as, one might add embarrassingly, to the economic crunch of many synagogues.[17]

The Reform constituency, on the other hand, having far less association with the *hazzanic* (cantorial) ways of the past, is relatively free of bias. A woman cantor on the pulpit is only a short step away from the soloist in the professional choir, except that now she is Jewish. And yet even here, when placement requests are made, one still hears apologetic hints that a male candidate should be preferred.

The one question that is least discussed, yet, objectively, has more validity for debate is that of the cultural integrity and authenticity of the *hazzanut* itself. Can, or should, a musical content, created and shaped out of the peculiarities of one particular instrument, be freely adopted by another instrument, of a totally different character?

Interestingly, this very same question is being argued about in general music circles with particular regard to Baroque literature and instruments.[18] Should the keyboard music of Bach, for example, which was composed for the clavichord, organ, or harpsichord, be performed on a contemporary piano?

Hazzanut, that vital musical heritage of our people, did, after all, develop its uniqueness out of the vocal distinctiveness and character of the male singer—the tenor no less. With a Bach prelude and fugue, one might argue that its musical substance is of such pure abstractness, that it loses nothing of its essence when played on a modern keyboard (many even say Bach would have eagerly accepted a well-tempered Steinway grand). But with *hazzanut*, simple transference from male to female voice is a different matter. The very heart of *hazzanut*—the indescribable earthiness, texture, taste, and pathos in need of a wide range of color and primitive-like ornamentation, deeply linked with the spontaneous outpouring of a male-*davening* congregation, chanted in a language that was almost exclusively reserved for men—should naturally and necessarily be bound up with the male voice.[19]

Oddly enough, because cantorial art became almost totally identified with the tenor voice, a remarkable phenomenon took place. Singers who, physiologically, possessed a deeper baritone or bass voice, instinctively and unconsciously "tenorized" their instruments, forcing their vocal system to take on a "tenorial" attitude, range, and style, most of the time convincingly. There are some of us who insist that even the great tenor Yossele Rosenblatt was a natural bass who miraculously transformed his instrument into that glorious tenor sound at the demands of the pervasive culture.[20]

It is because of all of the above that legitimate argument is expressed, justifiably, and without bias, by remnants of old-time purists who can accept *hazzanut* only on its original terms. At the same time, it becomes more understandable why Reform worshipers are freer to accept women, since most of them have never experienced the old cantorial culture. One should note, however, that occasionally we do hear a woman *hazzan* who has captured the quintessence of the old-fashioned way, but has done so because of two conditions: in-depth environmental influence from having been brought up in the old culture, and, most important, vocal adjustment by seriously favoring the so-called "chest voice" to the point when it approaches, downwardly, the tenor range and character. These are then some of the questions: Should a cantor sound like a singer or a *hazzan*? Are there not male cantors who are at best good singers, but who lack that "certain something," and at worst who pitifully attempt an imitation of what they superficially know as the real thing? Given the realities that it is a rarity to be able to live successfully in two worlds—modernity and the authenticity of the past—the least one could hope of cantors, male and female, is their honesty and sensitivity: honesty to one's natural resources (whatever voice one possesses), and, at the same time, sensitivity and respect for what is genuine in our musical tradition, even if it requires the sacrifice of some element of one's so-called "legitimate" vocal personality.

When congregants say, "He has a brilliant voice but it is too operatic for the synagogue," what they really mean is that he lacks the flexibility and warmth so important for the passionate sweetness of our cantorial tradition. When they say, "She has such a beautiful voice, it is like being at a concert," what they really mean is that she is demonstrating her expansive range of voice to the disadvantage of the character of *hazzanut* (words are seriously distorted in the higher range of a woman's voice). In either case, it is the humanity of the person that makes the difference.

To move or to impress, that is the question. If a *hazzan* is driven to be moved, as well as to move, he or she will be able to give up being impressive. Ultimately, it is the *person* that touches the congregant, not the baritone, contralto, tenor, or soprano; and when that happens, he or she will be genuinely identified as the *hazzan*.

21. GATES OF PRAYER*

I do not claim to be a presenter of critique, nor a presenter of solutions. I say this because when I confront myself these days with the seeking out of answers to the problems of the new

---

*Reprinted from the *Central Conference of American Rabbis 1976 Yearbook*, following the publication of the new Reform prayer book, *Gates of Prayer*.

liturgy of *Gates of Prayer*, no less the entire complex state of worship today, two responses come to my mind. The first one says that the answer is so simple and obvious that I would be embarrassed to speak of it. And the second one says that the problem is so vast, that it would be too overwhelming a task to take on, no less to solve.

It is unanswerable. And so it goes very likely with most of us that we know all the answers that are knowable, and we are frustrated by our quest for answers that cannot be known at this time.

Having nevertheless been drawn to this topic, I did begin to focus my thinking not on solutions themselves, but on some of the problems of solutions—the ones that are not knowable and the ones that are accessible. There are two areas of interest which I hope may be of some value to you. The first has to do with the unconscious inner process that a new liturgy must face before it can reach any living potential. It may be of comforting support to realize that the problem of confronting a new liturgy is an old one. In a curious way, we are probably coming to grips with a similar dynamics that our ancestors experienced during the development and the practice of the *siddur* (prayer book).

To begin with, both liturgies came into being out of an unnatural condition of having to solve a problem. That is, both the traditional *siddur* and the Reform *Gates of Prayer* were shaped not as a response to an established, living culture of prayer, but rather as an attempt to deal with a problem arising out of a radical change in conditions.[21] The specifics of change are, of course, quite different, but the purpose of the liturgies, to fill a void out of concern for preservation, is common to both periods. In the past, it was the void coming out of the collapse of Jerusalem and the Temple, which produced an essentially new concept of a Diaspora liturgy.[22] Today it is a similar void coming out of serious weakening of an existent institution of worship that has produced the new prayer book, in the hope that it would revitalize—and indeed preserve—the very institution that is now plagued by the absence of inner commitment to its inherent purpose.

Though both prayer books contain the potential ingredients for prayer, nevertheless, underlying their totality is this fundamental unnaturalness, an incongruity in terms of the worship realities at the times that they both emerged. It is therefore necessary to view them not in terms of what they were to begin with externally, literally, but what they would eventually become, how they would be transformed inwardly, experientially.

I see this process of becoming, developing out of an interplay between the known, external form and logic of the liturgy, and the ongoing, unconscious seeking of an inner form. While we would like very much to be able to put our fingers on the inner form, this cannot be, not only because it depends on the instinctive and the spontaneous, but also because it is dependent on the unknown of the potential worshiper of the future, what he himself will become.

The *siddur* with its accumulative character, its abundance of materials, with its sometimes clear lack of a total and integral unity of a piece, could not have survived without the evolution of an inner form and stream that ultimately helped transcend the objective ingredients, and thus come to dominate them.[23] Without this developing inner flow of orchestration and choreography of a host of elements, this *siddur*, for those who use it today, would have no living reality. This is not the time to try to detail some of the specifics of this inner form. Today we are faced with the same need for entering this critical process leading to an inner form, as we begin to introduce the *Gates of Prayer* in our services. The external mechanics in dealing with a new form and even the idiosyncrasies of a new prayer book can be left to commonsense guidelines. And I say this particularly since there is no single path that can satisfy our unusual state of diversity, something that I will address shortly.

The expanded and optional character of the prayer book, for example, will demand an extended period of experience and play before it will lose its self-conscious state so that ultimately the optional itself will no longer be experienced as the optional.

There may also exist another important aspect in the relationship between the fixed literal content of a liturgy and the functioning inner process. It is very conceivable that the more the liturgy itself presents problems toward realization, the more it demands intensification of the inner dynamics to cope with such problems. In the case of the *siddur*, it was not only the problem of its massive cumulative content, but equally the fact that it was fixed, unchanged, other than by addition, for a remarkably long period of time, that required an ongoing active inner process.[24] Without these dynamics, the *siddur* would have remained static to the point of deterioration and collapse. Ironically, then, we may want perhaps to view the difficulties that the *Gates of Prayer* poses for us as an advantage, in positive terms, because it will force us even more to create inwardly if it is to realize itself somewhere in the future. The *Gates of Prayer* as it is will not be with us for a very long period of time. We already are aware of the need for certain changes in its form and content that we may like to project onto an inevitable revised edition. It is perhaps fortunate that, because of economics, we will have to wait for such a revision, precisely because it will insist that we struggle with our own inner resources to transcend and to transform the idiosyncrasies of the material.

Now, what the actual inner form will be cannot be articulated. It will have to have its own life. There is, however, one fundamental that I feel must participate in this process if it is to progress at all. Transcendence is perhaps an old and tired concept for many of us. It has lost its force and vitality for many of us, and yet I am convinced that without its presence, nothing more than a secularized fragmented series of mere activities will come forth under the guise of worship, as it is already beginning to take place today. Transcendence of the objective limitations of the *Gates of Prayer* demands that we ourselves transcend, that we allow the instinctive to take over and dominate the liturgy and thus transform it.

I realize that we tend to attribute our difficulties with the idea of transcendence to the ever-increasing struggle with a God relationship.[25] While I know that this struggle is real for many of us, I want to suggest a possible reversal of cause and effect. That is, to consider seriously the possibility that for whatever historical, sociological, and psychological conditions that have affected us, that it is the very loss of our ability to transcend that has had an impact on our sense of God, or at least to say that we are caught up in a vicious circle whereby both cause and effect are feeding and weakening each other. Whether or not this notion holds true, I cannot foresee a serious quest for the inner form and transformation of the new prayer book without first entering the process ourselves. This has to do with the unknowable.

The second area that touches on the knowable deals with my hesitance to come up with concrete answers, and comes out of the unique conditions in which the individual cult of personalities—rabbis and cantors—find themselves today. To help understand this condition, I find it necessary to look at the relationship between the pulpit functionary and the worship experience during the much earlier and more stable period of worship.

During this period, when the experience of worship was more clearly defined, when worship had its own life and independent force, the individual, along with his peculiarities, was relatively submerged into this stream.[26] What I mean by the individual here is his personality makeup, his strengths, his limitations, his idiosyncrasies, be he more gregarious or more intellectual. The individual here could lose himself in the anchor of this dependable stream, to submit himself to the security of the existent, stable entity. His own individuality was secondary to the prime independence of *tefillah*. This held true as well for the congregations of that period, for the force of the total worship experience transcended much of the distinctive character that they possessed, producing a greater uniformity of manner and style of worship.[27]

Today, with the increased weakening and breakdown of stability and entity of worship, the individual now finds himself alone without the support of an entity, indeed, having to create an entity himself which now becomes more dependent on his own resources, so that his own distinctive personality comes to the fore and is called upon to direct the course taken by worship. The particular direction of exploration and experimentation when this does take place will, to a great extent, be influenced by the nature of each personality—what is right and natural for him or her.

This condition is, of course, clearly demonstrated by the vast diversity of manners and style of worship today.[28] This condition can produce a potential confusion among us as we search out for new ways and grope for answers that will help revitalize our services. This is particularly so when we are eager to revitalize our services, to receive new formulas offered by the innovator. The danger here lies in our ignoring the possibility that this or that *siddur* may have been shaped out of the unique personality makeup of a particular individual and/or his congregation, and to assume that it can be universally applied can be a troublesome oversimplification. What is right and natural for one innovator may be totally awkward and unworkable for another.

The only thing that I do suggest with regard to the idea of receiving ideas is that it is much more critical to search out the essence of the thing and less to seize upon the thing itself, to let the essence direct the reshaping of the thing into whatever way will more naturally reflect oneself.

22. TRAINING FOR A FUTURE IN DOUBT

The ideal cantorial graduate is not produced by a school catalog. An impressive curriculum has never interested me. A fancy list of courses is easy to print, but fulfilling it is another matter.

These words are particularly challenging today. Even if we had the freedom to create the ideal cantorial program, we would simply not know how to accomplish it. The question mark of the future, of what we will be, is an enormous one. No one can adequately respond to it. And yet if this is the case, what does one do? How does one train for an unknown?

One possible answer is that one makes a choice between making the most of what one has and paralysis. I have seen this choice made fifty years ago (in 1954), just as I see it made in our schools today.

Fifty years ago, our curriculum may have been limited, but it was not bad.[29] And yet I remember how superficial the relationship was of most of the men to what was offered. Those who entered with considerable background left with little more, while those who came with a meager background worked only as much as was necessary to distinguish themselves from their congregants as professionals. The exceptions were few.

The reasons for such a state are many, but I would like to focus upon two conditions that I feel contribute predominantly to our reaction of passivity. First is our reaction to the illiteracy and marginality of the laymen, and second, our reaction to the great doubt as to what the future will ask of us.

There are two ways in which a person can shape the scope and intensity of his development: he can do it himself or he can let others do it for him. He can determine his own growth through his own inner motivation, or he can allow it to be dictated by external influences. Our tendency today is to set the concept of our professional training in direct proportion to the level of those whom we serve. The more the layman is literate, the more the professional must be. The less knowledgeable the layman, the less knowledgeable the professional need be.[30] This proportion is achieved not only by the kind of demand made by the training institution upon the student but also by the student—and later, cantor—upon himself.

It is precisely because of this ratio that *hazzanut* developed so intensively as it did in our immediate past. When everyone is a *shikl chazan* (little cantor), then the *hazzan* himself must rise far beyond.[31] This deep and rich culture could never have emerged without the great literacy of the Eastern European masses. Today we are struggling to preserve *hazzanut*, yet we continue passively to be pulled under by those whom we serve. The difference of this unconscious "who would know the difference" must be confronted.

I have often wondered about the wisdom of supplying students of the school with pulpits. While we can all see the practical side of this, we nevertheless risk a student being placed in a situation where he may prematurely decide, consciously or otherwise, just what he needs to know as a cantor. The temptation to remain about one lesson ahead of them is much too dangerous. To be preoccupied with the question "Can I use it Friday night?" is to be deceived into superficial existence.

The second condition, which concerns me even more, is that of our reaction to doubt. I think all of us are plagued by a future that tells us very little. We face a remarkable blank. The synagogue itself is a question mark.[32] We have few seers today.

I am certain that most of us think we will exist twenty years from today, but as to what our specific role, character, musical lineage and so on will be is a monumental puzzlement. One very live witness to this is the Central Conference for American Rabbis' total helplessness to take even the first step toward a new liturgy.[33]

To compound our predicament, we now begin to doubt the validity of our entire traditional foundation for the future.[34] We begin to question the need to perpetuate our great tradition of the past: *nusach* (traditional chant), *hazzanut*, cantillation (chanting of the Hebrew Bible), the classics, even Hebrew. It is one thing to question the future, or even to question our past as some kind of base for the future, but it is another thing to break with it, to destroy the bridge, when this question is still a question, and when we are only in doubt and not convinced. The fact that I do not know what will happen in the future, the fact that I do not know what role tradition will play (if at all) does not give me the right to cut my ties with it. I may want to put some of my bridges into mothballs where they may be easily reached, but to burn them all may lead to irreparable consequences. How often have we regretted having burned our bridges prematurely?

The worst part of an enveloping doubt is not that it wants us to question the validity of specific ways in our present and for our future, but that it drains us of energy to act at all. Not only does it tempt us to deny our past, it also rejects any new and struggling glimpse at the future. We cannot wait for the future to clarify itself to us. Some of it may depend precisely on whether we do anything now. Those who have the ability to explore new worlds are to be praised, and those who cannot may still search for new meanings in the old. I still find great beauty in our past. As a matter of fact, I feel it is my dynamic tie with the wealth of our past that nourishes my openness to the new.

There is one final point that touches upon our fears about the future. With all that I have said, if our psyches are to center exclusively on the music of the synagogue, then we will surely become lost outsiders. We would find ourselves only a few steps away from the choir loft. Our dedication to our musical purpose must join with an expanding and newly discovered love and concern for our people. They need our concern as much as they need our chant. It is even conceivable that the more we enter the lives of our people, the more we may discover new paths for our musical tradition, paths that would emerge out of our total selves rather than out of ourselves as outsiders.

Glossary

Aggadah (also *Haggadah*) "Narration." Exegetical texts dealing with morals and lessons drawn from the Bible, found especially in *Talmud* and *Midrash*. Parables, theology, philosophy, lore, ethics, wisdom, and history are contained in *Aggadah*.

Aleinu "Let us Rise." The closing prayer in Jewish worship services.

Aliyah "Going up." A term used in the synagogue service for the honor extended to a worshiper who is called up to the *bima* (pulpit) to recite a blessing over the Torah.

Amen "So be it." An affirmative congregational response to a preceding statement. Generally corresponds to the modal structure of the preceding passage of liturgy.

Aramaic A 3,000-year-old Semitic language similar to Hebrew. Parts of the biblical books of Ezra and Daniel as well as sections of the two *Talmuds* and *Mishnah* were written in Aramaic. In the present day, the *ketubah* (Jewish marriage contract), *get* (Jewish writ of divorce) and the *Kaddish* (mourner's prayer) are written in Aramaic.

Ashkenazi Originally Jews from Germany, Ashkenazi Judaism migrated elsewhere in Central, Western, and Eastern Europe. Today the majority of world Jewry is Ashkenazi.

Ba'al Keriah (also *Ba'al Koreh*) "Master reader." In the synagogue setting, one who is responsible for the chanting, or *cantillation*, of the *Torah* scroll. The *ba'al keriah* is sometimes a professional position, but a cantor or layperson can also perform this function.

Ba'al Tefillah "Master of prayer." One who leads the congregation in prayer, often used interchangeably with *sheliach tzibbur* (messenger of the congregation). Typically a lay leader, as opposed to a professional cantor.

Ba'al Tekiah "Master blower." One who blows the *shofar* (ram's horn). Historically, the blowing of the *shofar* announced important public events. Today, the *ba'al tekiah* blows the *shofar* during the Hebrew month of *Elul*, on *Rosh Hashanah* (New Year), and *Yom Kippur* (Day of Atonement).

Bar/Bat Mitzvah "Son/daughter of commandment." A rite of passage coinciding with the thirteenth birthday, when a Jewish person is believed mature enough to take on the responsibilities of adulthood—namely the fulfillment of *mitzvot* (commandments). In preparation, the child studies the Bible, Talmud, Jewish law, ritual, and history. The central rite of the *bar/bat mitzvah* ceremony is the child's chanting from *Torah* and *Haftarah* (Prophetic Books), typically on Shabbat morning.

Bavli The *Talmud* of Babylonia, compiled around 500 C.E. *Talmud Bavli* contains *Mishnah* (commentary on the Pentateuch) and *Gemara* (commentary on *Mishnah*).

Berakhot "Blessings." Generally, *berakhot* begin with the formula, "Praised are You, Lord our God, King of the Universe."

Berit "Covenant."

Berit Milah "Covenant of Circumcision." A central *mitzvah* (commandment) in Judaism, it is a sign of the covenant between

God and man first reveled to Abraham. By custom, the Jewish male child is circumcised eight days after birth.

Bima "Pulpit." An elevated platform traditionally used as a desk for the chanting of the Torah. *Bima* can also refer generally to the "stage" on which the rabbi and cantor stand to lead worship.

Cantillation Modes used for the public chanting of the Hebrew Bible. Cantillation is the interpretation of *te'amim* ("tastes," or "chant marks") that accompany the printed text of the Hebrew Bible.

Cantor (Latin equivalent of *hazzan*.) "Singer." The solo singer in the synagogue who leads the congregation in prayer. A title appropriated from the German Protestant *kantor*, it was first used in the eighteenth century in lands where Romance languages were spoken.

Chukat Hagoy "Manner of the Gentiles." Refers to non-Jewish elements (particularly Christian) traditionally forbidden from the synagogue, such as music, rituals, and customs.

Conservative Judaism A liberal movement of Judaism developed in the United Sates during the twentieth century, which seeks to balance traditional Jewish ritual and law with the demands of the modern world.

Daven "To Pray." Eastern European Jews and their descendants use the word *daven* to refer generally to the act of prayer. Pious Jews *daven* thrice daily: evening (*ma'ariv*), morning (*shakharit*), and afternoon (*minkhah*), with added prayers for *Shabbat* and holidays.

Diaspora "Dispersion." Refers to Jews living outside of the Land of Israel.

Ethical Monotheism Belief in a single, all-powerful, just and merciful God who demands that people act decently toward one another.

Galut "Exile." Refers generally to Jews living outside of the Land of Israel. The first major exile occurred after the Babylonian destruction of the First Temple in Jerusalem (586 B.C.E. to 516 B.C.E.). The second exile began in 70 C.E., when the Romans conquered Judea. Related to *Diaspora*.

Halakhah The tradition of Jewish Law. *Halakhah* is derived from the root "walk," as in "walking with God." *Halakhah* contains legal decisions, guidance, practice, and is the foundation of traditional Jewish life. The rules of *Halakhah* are derived from *Talmud* (Oral Torah).

Hasidism "Pious Ones." An ecstatic form of Judaism founded by the Rabbi Israel Baal Shem Tov ("Master of the Good Name," 1700–60), which places primary importance on music. Hasidism considers its sacred music a vehicle for the attainment of inspiration, devotion, exaltation, and spiritual elevation.

Haskalah Jewish "Enlightenment." A rationalist movement that began in eighteenth-century Germany and spread elsewhere in Europe. The *Maskilim* ("Enlightened Ones") believed that differences that divided Jews and the majority culture—especially in the areas of language, dress, rituals, and customs—were responsible for their persecution, and that, by adopting modern European culture, Jews could assimilate and become fully emancipated citizens of Europe.

Havdalah "Separation." The closing ceremony of Shabbat. The *Havdalah* service marks the transition from sacred to mundane time. The *Havdalah* ceremony includes *berakhot* (blessings) over wine, *besamim* (spices), and a braided candle. Songs are usually sung following the ceremony.

Hazzan Cantor. Most scholars trace *hazzan* to the Hebrew root *hazah*, "to see." In Talmudic days, the *hazzan* was a general communal functionary, or overseer, of the congregation. Today the *hazzan*'s primary duty is to lead the congregation in the chanting and singing of prayers.

Hazzanut Cantorial art. Refers to "elevated" melodies sung by a *hazzan*, typically in a florid style. The term can also refer to regional styles, for example, Polish *hazzanut*, or German *hazzanut*. *Hazzanut* is characteristically emotive and commonly regarded as the height of Jewish sacred music.

Hebrew The language of the Jewish people since ancient times, in which most of the Bible and much of the postbiblical rabbinic literature is written. Traditionally the language of Scripture and liturgy, Hebrew has been revived in the modern state of Israel as a spoken language.

Hishtapkhut Hanefesh "Outpouring of the soul."

Hitlahavat Berash "Tumultuous enthusiasm."

Huppah Marriage canopy.

Jewishness The ethnic culture of Jews as a secular group, as opposed to a Jewish religious identity.

Kabbalat Shabbat "The ushering in of Shabbat." A collection of prayers recited and sung at the beginning of the Friday night Shabbat service. First introduced in the sixteenth century by *Kabbalists* in Sefad, Israel, *Kabbalat Shabbat* prayers include *Lekhu N'ran'na* ("Let Us Sing to the Lord"), and *Lekhah Dodi* ("Come My Beloved").

Kahal; Kehillah Jewish "community." A form of voluntary community organization, such as a congregation.

Karaism A medieval sect of Judaism that rejected the authority of rabbinic Judaism. Karaites believe that only the written Torah was revealed by God to Moses at Sinai. Though a small sect, there are several thousand Karaites in the world today.

Kavvanah "Intention." *Kavvanah* is the act of directing one's mind to pay close attention to the prayer or *mitzvah* he or she is performing. As a noun, *kavvanah* denotes meaning and purpose, or the state of complete awareness of what one is doing.

K'lal Yisrael "Jewish solidarity." The *mitzvah* (commandment) of uniting world Jewry in an expanded community, or family.

Klezmer From the Hebrew *klei-zemer*, meaning "Instruments of song." *Klezmer* is Eastern European Jewish folk and dance music, and refers to both a group of musicians and the music itself.

K'vod Hatzibbur "Respect for the Congregation."

Ladino Spanish-Jewish language. The traditional vernacular of *Sephardic* Jews. Essentially a mixture of medieval Spanish and Hebrew; also called Judeo-Spanish.

Ma'ariv The evening service, first of the three daily services (Jewish days begin at sundown).

Machzor Festival prayer book. Based on the *siddur* (weekday and Shabbat prayer book), but containing additional material, such as *piyyutim* (liturgical poetry).

Mavin "Expert," from the Hebrew root "to understand." A good judge of quality, or a connoisseur.

Megillah "Scroll." There are five scrolls contained in the Hebrew Bible: Song of Songs (*Shir Hashirim*), Ruth, Lamentations (*Eichah*), Ecclesiastes (*Kohelet*), and Esther.

Midrash, "Study" or "Exegesis." A collection of biblical exegeses, characterized by broad interpretation. The Talmud contains *Midrash Halakhah*, which deals with the meaning of biblical law, and *Midrash Aggaddah*, which draws moral principle from biblical accounts. Generally speaking, *Midrash* is an interpretation of Scripture by a rabbinic sage.

Minhag Jewish "custom." *Minhag* refers to local customs and traditions that have over time developed a binding character. Generally there is *Minhag Ashkenaz* (European custom) and *Minhag Sepharad* (Eastern custom).

Minyan Minimum quorum of ten Jewish adults over the age of thirteen required for public services. A *minyan* is required for the recitation of *Kaddish* (mourner's prayer) and for the reading of Torah. Traditionally, only men are counted in *minyanim*, though egalitarian liberal denominations count women among the ten.

Mishnah "Learning." Redacted in 200 c.e., *Mishnah* is the oldest postbiblical collection of Jewish laws. The *Mishnah* is a collection of oral laws derived from the Torah by rabbinic sages. It is composed of six sections (or, *sedarim*): 1) Seeds (*Zeraim*); 2) Festivals (*Moed*); 3) Women (*Nashim*); 4) Damages (*Nezikin*); 5) Holy Matters (*Kodashim*); 6) Purities (*Tohorot*).

Misinai tunes Melodies "from Mount Sinai." A corpus of melodies that originated in southwestern Germany between the eleventh to fifteenth centuries, which are prevalent in the High Holy Day and festival services of the Ashkenazi (European) tradition.

Mitzvah "Commandment." A religious and moral obligation required by God. In Jewish tradition, there are 613 *mitzvot*; 245 are positive, while 365 are negative.

Musaf "Addition." The additional service recited on Sabbaths and holidays, which replaces the additional sacrifice offered in Temple days.

Niggun Tune or "melody type." A wordless melody sung by the *Hasidim* (followers of *Hasidism*).

Nusach Traditional liturgical chant. Refers to specific melodic patterns or prayer modes used for worship. *Nusach* motives have no fixed meter, are subject to repetition, and allow for structured improvisation. Traditional *nusach* is specific to particular worship services, and various sections within the services.

Orthodox Judaism In modern times, Orthodoxy refers to traditional Judaism. Orthodox Jews consider both the *Torah* (Pentateuch) and *Talmud* ("Oral Torah") to be binding, and adhere to *Halakhah* (Jewish law).

Pesach "Passover." An eight-day springtime festival that commemorates the exodus of the children of Israel from Egyptian bondage; also referred to as "The Season of Freedom."

Piyyut Hebrew liturgical poetry. *Piyyutim* were composed largely during the Middle Ages and were added to Shabbat and holiday services. *Piyyutim* are usually sung.

Rabbi "My master." Originally an unofficial title, the office of the rabbinate was established in the Middle Ages. The Rabbi is the official religious and legal authority of the Jewish community.

Reconstructionism An American Jewish denomination that began in the twentieth century and conceives of Judaism as a "religious civilization," and not a religion exclusively. To the Reconstructionists, Judaism is a way of life based on religion, language, literature, customs, folkways, music, and art.

Reform Judaism A liberal movement of Judaism that began in Germany in the nineteenth century and is characterized by modern interpretations of Jewish ritual and law, and individual choice.

Rosh Hashanah Jewish "New Year." The first day of the month of *Tishrei*, *Rosh Hashanah* falls in September or October.

Seder "Order." The ceremony held in Jewish homes on the first two nights (or the first night only in Israel and among Reform Jews) of *Pesach* (Passover). The *seder* commemorates the Israelites' miraculous escape from Egyptian bondage.

Sephardic Originally Jews from Spain and Portugal, Sephardic Jews were expelled from their homelands during the Spanish and Portuguese Inquisitions (1492 and 1497), and migrated to Italy, Southern France, North Africa, and the Middle East. The traditional Sephardic language is *Ladino*, which is a mixture of Hebrew and medieval Spanish.

Shabbat Jewish Sabbath. Weekly day of rest, following the biblical injunction, "Remember the Sabbath day and keep it holy" (Exodus 20:8). *Shabbat* serves as a reminder of God's rest after the six days of Creation and is observed as a day of worship and rest. Shabbat begins Friday evening at sundown, and continues until sundown on Saturday.

Shakharit "Morning." The daily morning service.

Shalosh Regalim The three major pilgrimage festivals in Judaism: *Pesach* (Passover), *Shavuot* (Pentecost), and *Sukkot* (Feast of the Tabernacles). Following a biblical commandment, ancient Israelites would make a pilgrimage to the Temple in Jerusalem during these holidays.

Shavuot The festival of weeks; also referred to as Pentecost. Shavuot celebrates Moses' receiving of *Torah* at Mount Sinai. Shavuot comes fifty days after Passover.

Sheliach Tzibbur "Messenger of the congregation." The title *sheliach tzibbur* is applied to the person leading the congregation in prayer. While this can be a lay leader, the cantor is also called *sheliach tzibbur*.

Shema Yisrael "Hear O Israel." The first words of the proclamation of the monotheistic creed; also known as the watchword of the Jewish faith.

Shemini Atzeret The feast of conclusion on the eighth day of *Sukkot*.

Shoah "Vast Destruction." The Holocaust. The German Nazi murder of nearly 6 million Jews between 1933 and 1945.

Shofar Ram's horn. In biblical times, the *shofar* was blown to announce important events and occurrences: alarms during wartime, approaching Sabbath and festivals, ushering in national events. Today the *ba'al tekiah* (master blower) sounds the *shofar* during the Hebrew month of *Elul*, and particularly on *Rosh Hashanah* and *Yom Kippur*.

Shokhet Jewish ritual slaughterer, or butcher. The *shokhet* must be an observant Jew who follows the laws of *shehitah* (the slaughtering ritual), which is understood to be a quick and humane way to slaughter animals. The *shokhet* must have official certification from an Orthodox rabbi.

Shtetl "Small town"; in particular, the Jewish communities of Eastern Europe. Ashkenazi (European) Jewish culture flourished in the *shtetls*, which were prevalent prior to World War II.

Shtibel A small synagogue, or "prayer room." A simple, unpretentious room where a small group—typically not much larger than a *minyan*—gathers to pray communally.

Shuckling Swaying back and forth during prayer. *Shuckling* originated as a way to show awe and trembling before God, and to illustrate the flame of the soul.

Shul Synagogue, or "house of prayer." The *shul* is the center of Jewish education, worship, and communal life. In Hebrew, *shul* is called *bet knesset* (house of assembly), which is reflected in the Greek term *synagogue*, meaning "assembly," or "congregation."

Siddur From the Hebrew meaning "order." The *siddur* is the

Jewish prayer book. In addition to passages from the Bible, *siddurim* also include rabbinic wisdom, sacred poetry (*piyyutim*), prayer-songs (*zemirot*), contemporary readings, and other liturgical matter.

Simchat Torah "Rejoicing of the Torah." The day following *Shemini Atzeret*, *Simchat Torah* marks the completion of the annual cycle of Torah reading, and the beginning of a new cycle. The characteristic feature of the holiday is a series of processions in the synagogue (*hakkafot*) with the scrolls of the Torah.

Sinai The mountain on which God revealed the Torah to Moses.

Sofer "Scribe." Commonly applied to one who copies the Torah and other sacred texts onto scrolls of parchment.

Sukkot "Booths." The eight-day fall festival of *Sukkot* begins on the fifteenth day of *Tishrei* and commemorates the period when the Jews wandered in the wilderness and dwelt in *sukkot* (booths). The essential practice of the festival is dwelling in *sukkot* (booths), and waving the *lulav* (branches) and *etrog* (citrus fruit), which symbolize the agricultural nature of the holiday. Also known as the Feast of Tabernacles.

Synagogue From the Greek "to gather together." The main religious institution in Jewish life, the synagogue has a threefold purpose: house of public worship, house of study, and house of assembly. Also known as *bet knesset* (Hebrew) and *shul* (Yiddish).

Tallit A prayer shawl in which worshipers wrap themselves during the morning services. The *tallit* is rectangular in shape, made of silk or wool, with *tzitzit* (fringes) at each of the four corners.

Talmud "Study." A collection of religious-legal literature central to traditional Jewish life. Often called the "Oral Torah," it is second only to the Bible in its authority. The Talmud consists of *Mishnah*, the first code of laws after the Bible, and *Gemara*, an elaboration on the *Mishnah*.

Tanakh An acronym for the Hebrew Bible, derived from its three sections: *Torah* (Pentateuch), *Nevi'im* (Prophets), and *Ketuvim* (Writings).

Tefillah Jewish "Prayer." The Hebrew root for *tefillah* means variously "to think," "to judge," "to entreat," and "to intercede." Since the destruction of Jerusalem's Second Temple in 70 C.E., regular liturgical prayer has replaced Temple sacrifice as the way of Jewish worship. *Tefillah* may also refer to the prayerful atmosphere of worship, as in "a sense of *tefillah*."

Tefillin "Phylacteries." Two black leather cubes provided with long leather straps traditionally worn by Jewish males over the age of thirteen during the daily morning prayers (except on Sabbaths and holidays). The cases contain four passages from the Pentateuch written on parchment, and are placed on the bicep (*shel yad*) and head (*shel rosh*).

Torah "Religious instruction," or "learning." The first five books of the Hebrew Bible, or Pentateuch: Genesis (*Bereishit*), Exodus (*Shemot*), Leviticus (*Vayikrah*), Numbers (*Bamidbar*), and Deuteronomy (*Devarim*). More generally, *Torah* refers to the entirety of the Hebrew Bible and *Talmud*.

Yamim Nora'im "Days of Awe." The ten days beginning with *Rosh Hashanah* (New Year) and ending with *Yom Kippur* (Day of Atonement). During this period, Jews are judged spiritually for their deeds in the past year, and are inscribed in the Book of Life for the year to come.

Yerushalmi The *Talmud* of Jerusalem, completed around 400 C.E. *Talmud Yerushalmi* contains *Mishnah* (code of law) and *Gemara* (commentary on Mishnah). *Talmud Yerushalmi* is not as widely used as its Babylonian counterpart. Also known as the *Palestinian Talmud*.

Yiddish A language that was spoken widely by the Jews of Europe, but has essentially vanished as the Jewish vernacular since World War II. Yiddish is a combination of Middle High German and Hebrew.

Yom Kippur "Day of Atonment." The tenth day of the Hebrew month of *Tishrei*, occurring in autumn. *Yom Kippur* is a day of fasting, forgiveness, and confession of sin.

Yom Tov "Good Day." Jewish festival or holiday.

Zionism A political movement that aimed to create a Jewish national homeland in Palestine. The movement gained international recognition in 1917 with the Brittish Balfour Declaration and achieved its goal with the establishment of the State of Israel in 1948.

Zmirot Shabbat "songs" or "hymns." Jewish liturgical melodies typically borrowed from Jewish and non-Jewish folk traditions, and used primarily to express the joy of Shabbat and the exaltation of God. *Zmirot* are typically simple, lively melodies sung in unison by the congregation or around a dining table during Shabbat or holidays.

Endnotes

INTRODUCTION

1. See Peter Berger, *A Rumor of Angels: Modern Society and the Rediscovery of the Supernatural* (New York: Doubleday, 1969), pp. 52–75.

2. Ibid., p. 62.

3. Ibid., p. 60.

4. For discussion of the debate over Adolf Eichmann and his eventual execution, see the 1963 study, Hannah Arendt, *Eichmann in Jerusalem: A Report on the Banality of Evil* (New York: Penguin Classics Edition, 1994).

5. Berger, *A Rumor of Angels*, pp. 70–71.

6. One of the authors of this essay, Brad Stetson, is fully deaf in one ear, and partially deaf in the other, and has experienced this fear.

7. Robert S. Ellwood, *Introducing Religion from Inside and Outside*, 2nd ed. (Upper Saddle River, NJ: Prentice Hall, 1983), p. 110.

8. Jonathan Sacks, www.chiefrabbi.org/articles/ljnjt/yomkippur.htm., accessed January 12, 2007.

As Sacks suggests, certainly music has enhanced the ability of Judaism to survive throughout millennia in Diaspora, and not only music in the context of the synagogue, but also music in the context of the Jewish family. We should note that family, then, as the locus of socialization and a primary preservative of religious identity, should always be remembered as centrally important to the maintenance of both interpersonal and noetic religious practices.

9. Dale A. Matthews, M.D. with Connie Clark, *The Faith Factor: Proof of the Healing Power of Prayer* (New York: Viking, 1998), p. 45.

10. See Cynthia Davis, "The effects of music and basic relaxation instruction on pain and anxiety of women undergoing in-office gynecological procedures," *Journal of Music Therapy* 24, no. 4 (1992): 202–16.

11. Suzanne B. Hanser, "Music therapy and stress reduction research," *Journal of Music Therapy* 12, no. 4 (1985): 193–206.

12. See A. R. Laswell, "The Effects of Music Assisted Relaxation on the Relaxation, Sleep Quality, and Daytime Sleepiness of Sheltered, Abused Women." Unpublished master's thesis, Florida State University, 2000.

13. S. L. Robb et al., "The effects of music assisted relaxation on preoperative anxiety," *Journal of Music Therapy* 32, no. 1 (1995): 2–21. See also the popular discussion of music's manifold stress-reducing abilities in "Sing Out, Sister," *Los Angeles Times,* 23 April, 2007, p. F1.

14. On this idea generally, see Matthews, *The Faith Factor* (New York: Penguin, 1999), with its plethora of references, and the classic study by Herbert Benson, M.D., with Miriam Z. Klipper, *The Relaxation Response* (New York: Avon Books, 1979).

CHAPTER 1

1. Martin Stokes, ed., *Ethnicity, Identity and Music: The Musical Conception of Place* (New York: Berg Publishers 1994), p. 5.

2. Irene Heskes, *Passport to Jewish Music* (New York: Tara Publications, 1994), p. 116.

3. Jacob Neusner, ed., *Understanding Jewish Theology: Classical Issues and Modern Perspectives* (New York: Ktav Publishing, 1973), p. 262.

4. Nathan Glazer, *American Judaism* (Chicago: University of Chicago Press, 1957), p. 6.

5. Heskes, *Passport to Jewish Music,* p. 66.

6. Fabio Dasilva et al., *The Sociology of Music* (Notre Dame: University of Notre Dame Press, 1984), p. 80. Dasilva further explains the convergence of religion and music: "As in religion, where an idea or experience such as prayer is a direction rather than an experience of the Divine, in music a mode of consciousness can be reached that cannot be judged simply through empirical methods."

7. Rudolf Otto, *The Idea of the Holy* (London: Oxford University Press, 1923), p. 30.

8. Ibid., p. 151.

9. See Jennifer Robinson, "The Expression and Arousal of Emotion in Music," in *Musical Worlds: New Directions in the Philosophy of Music,* ed. Philip Alperson (University Park: Pennsylvania State University Press, 1998), pp. 13–22.

10. William James, *Varieties of Religious Experience* (New York: Mentor, 1958), p. 66.

11. Irene Heskes, ed., *Studies in Jewish Music: Collected Writings of A. W. Binder* (New York: Bloch Publishing, 1971), p. 183.

12. Leonard B. Meyer, *Emotion and Meaning in Music* (Chicago: University of Chicago Press, 1958), p. 24.

13. Oskar Sohngen, "Music and Theology: A Systematic Approach," in *Sacred Sound: Music in Religious Thought and Practice,* ed. Joyce Irwin (Chico, CA: Scholars Press, 1983), p. 8.

14. Dwight L. Bolinger, *The Symbolism of Music* (Yellow Springs, Ohio: Antioch Press, 1941), p. 27.

15. Roger W. H. Savage, "Music and Cultural Imagination," in *Selected Reports in Ethnomusicology*, vol. X (Los Angeles: UCLA Department of Ethnomusicology, 1994), p. 27.

16. Mark Slobin, *Chosen Voices: The Story of the American Cantorate* (Chicago: University of Illinois Press, 2002), p. 296.

17. Reuven Hammer, *Entering the High Holidays: A Guide to the Origins, Themes, and Prayers* (Philadelphia: Jewish Publication Society, 1998), p. 108.

18. Ibid., p. 116.

19. Translation from *Gates of Repentance: The New Union Prayer Book for the Days of Awe* (New York: Central Conference of American Rabbis, 1978), p. 252.

20. Joseph Telushkin, *Jewish Literacy* (New York: William Morrow and Company, 1991), p. 568.

21. Abraham Joshua Heschel, *God in Search of Man: A Philosophy of Judaism* (New York: Harper & Row, 1955), p. 314. Heschel continues: "*Kavanah*, then, is more than paying attention to the text of the liturgy or to the performance of the mitzvah. *Kavanah* is attentiveness to God. Its purpose is to direct the heart rather than the tongue or the arms. It is not an act of the mind that serves to guide the external action, but one that has a meaning in itself."

22. Heskes, *Passport to Jewish Music*, p. 117.

23. Erich Fromm, *Psychoanalysis and Religion* (New York: Bantam Books, 1950), p. 49.

24. Steven W. Dress, "K-Date: The Embrace of Keva and Kavannah in the Conservative Synagogue," in *United Synagogue Review* (spring/summer 2006): 25.

25. Jacob Neusner, *Israel in America: A Too Comfortable Exile?* (Boston: Beacon Press, 1985), p. 40.

26. Ibid., p. 39.

27. Abraham Joshua Heschel, *The Insecurity of Freedom* (New York: Farrar, Straus and Giroux, 1966), p. 244.

28. Ibid.

29. Ibid., p. 247.

30. Ibid.

31. Heather Robinson, "The New Cantor," *Reform Judaism* (winter 2003): 24.

32. Joan L. Roccasalvo, "The 'Sacred' in Sacred Music," *America* 28 (October 1995): 20.

33. Heschel, *Insecurity of Freedom*, p. 248.

34. See Shlomo Carlebach, *The Shlomo Carlebach Songbook* (New York: Zimrani Publishers, 1970).

35. Heschel, *Insecurity of Freedom*, p. 249.

36. Jeffery A. Summit, *The Lord's Song in a Strange Land: Music and Identity in Contemporary Jewish Worship* (New York: Oxford University Press, 2000), p. 89.

37. Ibid., p. 113.
38. Ibid., p. 48.
39. Robert N. Bellah et al., *Habits of the Heart: Individualism and Commitment in American Life* (Berkeley: University of California Press, 1985), p. 232.
40. Heschel, *Insecurity of Freedom*, p. 250.
41. Ibid., p. 251.
42. Ibid., p. 243.

CHAPTER 2

1. See Abraham Z. Idelsohn, *Jewish Music: Its Historical Development* (New York: Henry Holt and Co., 1929).

2. For discussions of how freedom and secularity have shaped American Judaism, see Jenna Weissman Joselit, *The Wonders of America: Reinventing Jewish Culture, 1880–1950* (New York: Henry Holt and Co., 1994), and Jacob Neusner, *American Judaism: Adventures in Modernity* (Englewood Cliffs, NJ: Prentice Hall, 1972).

3. For a lucid introduction to Jewish prayer, see Hayim Halevy Donin, *To Pray as a Jew: A Guide to the Prayer Book and the Synagogue Service* (New York: Basic Books, 1991).

4. Abraham Joshua Heschel treats the issue of private worship in his essay "On Prayer," which appeared in *Conservative Judaism* XXV, no. 1 (1970).

5. See "Minyan" in Joseph Telushkin, *Jewish Literacy* (New York: William Morrow and Company), pp. 643–44.

6. See Macy Nulman, *Concepts of Jewish Prayer and Music* (New York: Yeshiva University, 1985).

7. Abraham Joshua Heschel similarly favors the spontaneity of prayer. For example, see "Spontaneity is the Goal," in his book *Man's Quest for God: Studies in Prayer and Symbolism* (New York: Charles Scribner's Sons, 1954), pp. 48–89.

8. Also, it is imperative that congregants do not disturb each other when praying. See Abraham Stone's essay "Voice Level in Tefillah," in *Essays of Jewish Music and Prayer*, ed. Macy Nulman (New York: Yeshiva University, 2005), pp. 185–89.

9. For translations, origins, and meanings of many Jewish prayers, see Bernard Martin, *Prayer in Judaism* (New York: Basic Books, 1968).

10. For more on the emotional response to cantorial singing, see "The Golden Age of Cantorial Art," in Irene Heskes, *Passport to Jewish Music: Its History, Traditions, and Culture* (New York: Tara Publications, 1994), pp. 56–68.

11. Historically, liberal Judaism has viewed nonunison worship as undignified and disorderly, favoring instead the standards of Western decorum. See Eugene B. Borowitz and Naomi Patz, *Explaining Reform Judaism* (West

Orange, NJ: Behrman House, 1985), and Leon A. Jick, *The Americanization of the Synagogue, 1820–1870* (Hanover, NH: Brandeis, 1976).

12. See "Song of the Hazan," in Judith Kaplan Eisenstein, *Heritage of Music* (New York: UAHC, 1973), pp. 37–43.

13. During the "golden age" of *hazzanut* (cantorial art) (1910–40), concerts and recordings of the great cantors were very popular. The cantor who best exemplifies this period was Yossele Rosenblatt. For a biography, see Samuel Rosenblatt, *Yossele Rosenblatt: The Story of His Life as Told by His Son* (New York: Farrar, Straus and Young, 1954).

14. For more on the difficulties of prayer for modern Jews, see Jakob J. Petuchowski, *Understanding Jewish Prayer* (New York: Ktav Publishing, 1972), and Jacob Neusner, *Israel in America: A Too Comfortable Exile?* (Boston: Beacon Press, 1985).

15. See, for example, Shefton D. Temkin, *Creating American Reform Judaism: The Life and Times of Isaac Mayer Wise* (Oxford: Littman Library of Jewish Civilization, 1998), and Michael A. Meyer, *Response to Modernity: A History of the Reform Movement in America* (Detroit: Wayne State University Press, 1995).

16. Solomon Sulzer (1804–90) is often referred to as "father of the modern cantorate," and was the first to add Western harmonic coloring to traditional synagogue melodies and responses. See Macy Nulman, *Concise Encyclopedia of Jewish Music* (New York: McGraw-Hill, 1975), pp. 240–41, and Abraham Z. Idelsohn, *Jewish Music: Its Historical Development* (New York: Henry Holt, 1929), pp. 246–60.

17. See "The Influence of Moderate Reform Upon Synagogue Song During the Nineteenth Century in Central and Western Europe," in Idelsohn, *Jewish Music*, pp. 246–95.

18. The introduction of choir and organ into the Reform service was met with great controversy. See Jonathan D. Sarna, "The Question of Music in American Judaism," *American Jewish History* (June 2003): 195–204.

19. Louis Lewandowski (1821–94), like Sulzer, was instrumental in modernizing synagogue music. See Nulman, *Concise Encyclopedia of Jewish Music*, pp. 152–53.

20. See Macy Nulman, *The Encyclopedia of Jewish Prayer* (Northvale, NJ: Jason Aronson, 1993).

21. See Nachman T. Gidal, *Jews in Germany: From Roman Times to the Weimar Republic* (Köhn, Germany: Könemann, 1998).

22. Russian-Polish Cantor Abraham Ber Birnbaum (1865–1922) composed numerous settings for liturgical, folk, and art music. For biographical information, see Nulman, *Concise Encyclopedia of Jewish Music*, pp. 35-36.

23. For a sociohistorical analysis of Jewish denominational choice in America, see Bernard Lazerwitz et al., *Jewish Choices: American Jewish Denominationalism* (New York: State University of New York Press, 1998).

24. Secularity and ethnic needs have, in many cases, replaced religiosity among modern American Jews. This is exemplified in the levels of religious identification among Jewish celebrities. See, for example, Alan King et al., *Matzo Balls for Breakfast, and Other Memories of Growing Up Jewish* (New York: Free Press, 2004), and Abigail Pogrebin, *Stars of David: Prominent Jews Talk about Being Jewish* (New York: Broadway Books, 2005).

25. For more on the current trend of congregational singing in the synagogue, see Jeffery A. Summit, *The Lord's Song in a Strange Land: Music and Identity in Contemporary Jewish Worship* (New York: Oxford University Press, 2000).

26. See Neil Gillman, *Conservative Judaism: The New Century* (West Orange, NJ: Behrman House, 1993).

27. See Jacob Rader Marcus and Abraham J. Peck, *The American Rabbinate* (New York: Ktav Publishing House, 1985).

28. The Young Israel movement is a branch of Modern Orthodoxy aimed at stimulating youth involvement in Jewish worship, largely through congregational song. See "The Role of Liturgical Music in the Young Israel Movement," in Macy Nulman, *Concepts of Jewish Prayer and Music* (New York: Yeshiva University, 1985), pp. 91–92.

29. For the essays of two prominent Reform composers of the period— A. W. Binder (1895–1966) and Herbert Fromm (1905–95)—see Irene Heskes, ed., *Studies in Jewish Music: Collected Writings of A. W. Binder* (New York: Bloch Publishing, 1971), and Herbert Fromm, *On Jewish Music: A Composer's View* (New York: Bloch Publishing, 1978).

30. For more on the diversity of opinion surrounding belief and practice among Reform Jews, see Dana Kaplan, *Contemporary Debates in American Reform Judaism* (New York: Routledge, 2001), and Aron Harit-Manheimer, ed., *The Jewish Condition: Essays on Contemporary Judaism Honoring Rabbi Alexander M. Schindler* (New York: Union of American Hebrew Congregations, 1995).

31. "Instant spirituality" is a characteristic element of postmodern secular culture. See, for example, Robert Wuthnow, *After Heaven: Spirituality in America Since the 1950s* (Berkeley: University of California Press, 1998), and Richard Cimino and Don Lattin, *Shopping for Faith: American Religion in the New Millennium* (San Francisco: Jossey-Bass, 1998).

32. "Kid-friendly" liturgical songs, originally used for youth education, play an important role in the contemporary cantorate. See Heather Johnson, "The New Cantor," in *Reform Judaism* (Winter 2003): 23-28, 44, 74-76.

33. See "Music in the New State," in Marsha Bryan Edelman, *Discovering Jewish Music* (Philadelphia: Jewish Publication Society, 2003), pp. 221–48.

34. The response *Amen* ("So be it") has great value in Jewish tradition. The Talmud ("Oral Torah") teaches that, instead of singing or reciting an entire prayer, a congregant may—and in some cases *should*—simply respond

with *Amen*. See "Amen: A Verbal and Musical Response," in Macy Nulman, *Concepts of Jewish Prayer and Music* (New York: Yeshiva University, 1985), pp. 83–87.

35. See "Separating from Shabbat: The Havdalah Service," in Mark Dov Shapiro, *Gates of Shabbat: A Guide for Observing Shabbat* (New York: CCAR Press, 1996), pp. 61–70.

36. Rabbi Abraham Isaac Kook (1864–1935) was the first chief rabbi of Palestine (pre-state Israel), and was both an Orthodox mystic and progressive universalist. See, for example, Ben Zion Bokser, trans., *The Essential Writings of Abraham Isaac Kook* (Teaneck, NJ: Ben Yehudah Press, 2006).

CHAPTER 4

1. Conversation held on February 18, 2006, at Cantor William Sharlin's home.

2. Cantor Sharlin was born January 7, 1920. His parents and grandparents were settlers in pre-state Palestine, when the land was under Ottoman Turkish rule. For historical context, see Eugene R. Rogan, *Frontiers of the State in the Late Ottoman Empire: Transjordan, 1850–1921* (New York: Cambridge University Press, 2002).

3. Such diversification of Jewish identity has led to a nonessentialist approach in academia, which views Judaism as a heterogeneous and loosely defined category. The pervasive and transforming phenomena of acculturation, assimilation, and denominationalism have made Judaism (and other religious traditions) difficult to speak of in broad terms. According to Jacob Neusner, at any given time there may be competing "Judaisms," or a dominant system, but each requires individual examination. See Jacob Neusner, *Israel and Its Social Metaphors: Israel in the History of Jewish Thought* (Cambridge: Cambridge University Press, 1989), and Michael L. Satlow, "Defining Judaism: Accounting for 'Religions' in the Study of Religion," in *Journal of the American Academy of Religion* 74, no. 4 (2006): 837–60.

4. For an in-depth study of anglo-conformity, the "melting pot," cultural pluralism and generational changes in America, see Milton Myron, *Assimilation in American Life: The Role of Race, Religion, and National Origins* (New York: Oxford University Press, 2002).

5. This attitude is encapsulated in "Hansen's Law," inspired by immigration history pioneer William Lee Hansen's appraisal of the third generation: "What the son forgets, the grandson wishes to remember." See William Lee Hansen's books *The Immigrant in American History* (Cambridge: Harvard University Press, 1940), and *The Atlantic Migration, 1607–1860: A History of the Continuous Settlement of the United States* (New York: Harper Torchlight, 1961).

6. Over the last half century, intermarriage has become an increasing and oftentimes problematic reality of American Jewish life. Before 1965, 10

percent of Jews who married did so outside of the faith. Since 1985, that number has increased to 52 percent. This phenomenon has inspired a number of studies, symposiums, and books, including Anita Diamant, *Choosing a Jewish Life: A Handbook for People Converting to Judaism and for Their Family and Friends* (New York: Schocken, 1998).

7. Divorce is discouraged and oftentimes difficult in traditional Judaism. In the Talmud it is written that "Even [God] sheds tears when anyone divorces his wife" (Sanhedrin 22a). In order to divorce, the couple must receive a *get* (divorce document) from a rabbinic court, which annuls the *ketubah* (marriage contract).

8. The conflicting views on synagogue practice between the Orthodox and Reform denominations is explored in Ammiel Hirsch and Yaakov Yosef Reinman, *One People, Two Worlds: A Reform Rabbi and an Orthodox Rabbi Explore the Issues That Divide Them* (New York: Schocken, 2002). Stated succinctly, "It is impossible for American Reform Jews to imagine ritual and services, temple administration and clergy without the participation of women. More and more, our rabbis and cantors come from our female population. Then we look across the gulf at the world of the Orthodox and see an institutionalized attitude toward women that speaks more of an alien religion than a sect of its own" (pp. 47–48).

9. In the words of Marsha Bryan Edelman, "*Nusach* (traditional chant) had provided a form and structure to synagogue ritual, helping to define the Jewish seasons. In addition, despite general regional variations, the homogeneity of Ashkenazic musical tradition guaranteed that travelers—or displaced populations—could find accustomed rituals anywhere they went. The abrogation of time-honored Jewish liturgical practices created musical anarchy, with little of serious enough quality to compensate for the loss of spiritual succor once offered by familiar tunes." Marsha Bryan Edelman, *Discovering Jewish Music* (Philadelphia: Jewish Publication Society, 2003), p. 56.

10. The connection between the modern "problem of prayer" and synagogue music is noted in Abraham Joshua Heschel's essay, "The Vocation of the Cantor" in his book *The Insecurity of Freedom* (New York: Farrar, Straus and Giroux, 1966).

11. The absence of a deeply felt prayer experience falls into the larger discomfort with which liberal Jews approach ritual and belief. David Mamet explains, "These ceremonies, where they still exist, are subject to discount by the unbeliever, the dissatisfied, the intellectual." David Mamet, *The Wicked Son: Anti-Semitism, Self-Hatred, and the Jews* (New York: Schocken, 2006), p. 90.

12. The phenomenon of the "pop" service is not unique to the synagogue. Various Christian observers have also viewed contemporary trends in sacred music as an insufficient solution to the lack of inherent prayerfulness among worshipers. See, for instance, Albert L. Blackwell, *The Sacred in Music* (Louisville: Westminster John Knox Press, 1999).

13. The contemporary synagogue has in many ways become a place of casual, social gathering. Without the inclination to pray, synagogue-goers view more and more the worship service as a recreational event. Robert Wuthnow notes a similar phenomenon in America's mainline Protestant churches. See, for instance, his epilogue in *Christianity in the 21st Century: Reflections on the Challenges Ahead* (New York: Oxford University Press, 1993), pp. 213–17.

14. Jakob Petuchowski has reflected on the importance of the Hebrew worship service, and has expressed concern regarding its possible demise: "Without a Hebrew worship service, it is extremely doubtful whether even a minimal knowledge of the bare mechanics of Hebrew reading would have survived the vicissitudes of diaspora existence outside of a rather limited scholarly class. By conducting their worship in Hebrew, the Jews, as it were, saved their erstwhile national language from total extinction." Jakob J. Petuchowski, *Understanding Jewish Prayer* (New York: Ktav Publishing House, 1972), p. 45.

15. Arnold Eisen cites three principal challenges facing Jewish identity in America: 1) The loss of an integral community united around sacred text; 2) The rationalizing or marginalizing of belief due to scientific and historical consciousness; and 3) Little patience or need for the "truths" of Jewish tradition. Arnold M. Eisen, *Taking Hold of Torah: Jewish Commitment and Community in America* (Bloomington: Indiana University Press, 1999), p. 4.

16. Will Herberg expressed a similar concern: "The young Jew for whom the Jewish immigrant-ethnic group has lost all its meaning, because he was an American and not a foreigner, could think of himself as a Jew, because to him being Jewish now meant identification with the Jewish religious community." Will Herberg, *Protestant-Catholic-Jew: An Essay in American Religious Sociology* (Garden City, NY: Free Press), p. 187.

17. In some cases, assimilation has also led to Jewish self-hatred. The definitive study on this issue is Sander L. Gilman, *Jewish Self-Hatred: Anti-Semitism and the Hidden Language of the Jews* (Baltimore: Johns Hopkins University Press, 1986).

18. Cantor Sharlin earned a master's degree in composition from Manhattan School of Music.

19. This reflects the view that prayer's absolute requirement is *kavvanah*: focus, purposefulness, and devotion. Andrew Vogel Ettin, *Speaking Silences: Stillness and Voice in Modern Thought and Jewish Tradition* (Charlottesville: University of Virginia Press, 1994), p. 184.

20. For an in-depth study into the purpose and varieties of musical repetition, see Adam Ockelford, *Repetition in Music: Theoretical and Metatheoretical Perspectives* (Burlington, VT: Ashgate Publishing, 2005).

21. The larger folk movement of the 1960s and 1970s inspired simplistic congregational song in the American synagogue and summer camps. For more on the general cultural milieu, see Ronald D. Cohen, *Rainbow Quest:*

The Folk Music Revival and American Society, 1940–1970 (Amherst: University of Massachusetts Press, 2002).

22. This reflects a critique presented by Jewish Humanist rabbi Daniel Friedman: "Today most Jews are not religious. They may observe a Jewish holiday once in a while, although even when they do, it's more to express their Jewishness—their membership in the Jewish people—than to 'practice' Judaism." Daniel Friedman, *Jews Without Judaism: Conversations with an Unconventional Rabbi* (Amherst, NY: Prometheus Books, 2002), p. 26.

CHAPTER 5

1. For an analysis of the problems of Jewish assimilation, see Barry Rubin, *Assimilation and Its Discontents* (New York: Times Books, 1995).

2. Some have criticized "Holocaust-consciousness" as a substitute for authentic Jewish identity—that is, an identity in which religiosity is replaced with reverence for the martyrs of the Holocaust. For example, see Michael Goldberg, *Why Should Jews Survive?: Looking Past the Holocaust Toward a Jewish Future* (New York: Oxford University Press, 1995).

3. In traditional synagogue music, an important safeguard against the domination of foreign elements has been the use of synagogue modes. The principal modes are *Adonai Malach* ("The Lord Reigns"); *Magein Avot* ("Our Forbearer's Shield"); and *Ahavah Rabbah* ("With Abounding Love"). See "The Concept of Mode in European Synagogue Chant," in Hanoch Avenary, *Encounters of East and West in Music* (Tel-Aviv: Tel-Aviv University, 1979), pp. 86–96.

4. For readings on the diversification of the modern synagogue, see Jack Wertheimer, ed., *The American Synagogue: A Sanctuary Transformed* (Hanover, NH: Brandeis University Press, 1995).

5. For more on the problems of prayer in modern Judaism, see Jack J. Cohen, *Major Philosophers of Jewish Prayer in the Twentieth Century* (New York: Fordham University Press, 2000).

6. See Eric Werner, *From Generation to Generation: Studies on Jewish Musical Tradition* (New York: American Conference of Cantors, 1967).

7. The history of the cantorate has been colored by various personalities, styles, and fads. See Leo Landman, *The Cantor: An Historical Perspective* (New York: Yeshiva University, 1972).

8. For a brief discussion of the tensions between traditional and contemporary musical styles in the American synagogue, see "A Joyful Noise: Will much of Jewish music's beauty and history be lost as it adapts to the needs of the contemporary congregant?," in *Jewish Journal of Greater Los Angeles* 12 (May 2000): 9–10.

9. For more on the music of presentation and participation in the synagogue, see Mark Slobin, *Chosen Voices: The Story of the American Cantorate* (Chicago: University of Illinois Press, 2002), pp. 195–255.

10. For more on the cantor's role in the early American synagogues, see Leon A. Jick, *The Americanization of the Synagogue, 1820–1870* (Hanover, NH: Brandeis University Press, 1976).

11. Much has been written about the need for *kavvanah* (spiritual attentiveness) during prayer. For example, see Elliot N. Dorff, *Prayer for the Perplexed* (Los Angeles: University of Judaism, 1982), Jakob J. Petuchowski, *Understanding Jewish Prayer* (New York: Ktav Publishing, 1972), and Abraham Joshua Heschel, *God in Search of Man: A Philosophy of Judaism* (New York: Harper & Row, 1955), pp. 314–19.

12. See "Nostalgia as Jewish Mitzvah," in Arnold M. Eisen, *Rethinking Modern Judaism: Ritual, Commandment, Community* (Chicago: University of Chicago Press, 1998), pp. 156–87.

CHAPTER 6

1. Rabbinic Judaism maintains that Moses received both the Written Torah and Oral Torah (*Talmud*) from God at Mount Sinai (*Talmud Jerusalemi*, Pe'ah 2:6, 17a.); and "Moses received the Torah from Sinai and transmitted it to Joshua" (*Avot* 1:1). For an analysis of the historical Moses, see Jonathan Kirsch, *Moses: A Life* (New York: Ballantine Books, 1998).

2. From the prayer *Ahavah Rabbah* ("With Abounding Love").

3. Psalm 96: "Sing to the Lord a new song, sing to the Lord, all the earth," *Tanakh: The Holy Scriptures* (Philadelphia: Jewish Publication Society, 1985), p. 1222.

4. See R. Heber Newton, *The Mysticism of Music* (New York: G. P. Putnam, 1915).

5. The Ba'al Shem Tov (1698–1760) said, "A soul could not soar without melody." See Irene Heskes, *Passport to Jewish Music: Its History, Traditions, and Culture* (New York: Tara Publications, 1994), p. 119.

6. Within liturgy itself, there is a conflict between *keva* (tradition; routine) and *kavvanah* (spontaneity; intentionality). These polarities must be balanced in order to preserve tradition and to bring vitality to prayer. For treatments of this issue, see Seth Kadish, *Kavvana: Directing the Heart in Jewish Prayer* (Northvale, NJ: Jason Aronson, 1997), "Spontaneity and Tradition," in Jakob J. Petuchowski, *Understanding Jewish Prayer* (New York: Ktav Publishing House, 1972), pp. 3–16, and Steven W. Dress, "K-Date: The Embrace of *Keva* and *Kavannah* in the Conservative Synagogue," *United Synagogue Review* (spring/summer 2006): 24–26.

7. For the most part, *midrashic* literature explains the biblical text from an ethical-devotional point of view. See Jacob Neusner, *The Midrash: An Introduction* (Northvale, NJ: Jason Aronson, 1990), and Simi Peters, *Learning to Read Midrash* (Jerusalem: Urim Publications, 2005).

8. *Aggadah* "includes everything in Talmudic literature that is *not* of a

legal nature, such as descriptions of historical events and legends, proverbs and aphorisms that illustrate moral duties, and scientific data concerning medicine, mathematics, astronomy, physiology, botany and other branches of knowledge." Philip Birnbaum, *Encyclopedia of Jewish Concepts* (New York: Hebrew Publishing company, 1979), pp. 16–17. See also Avigdor Shinan, *The World of the Aggadah* (Tel Aviv: Mod Books, 1997).

9. For more on the content and development of the *siddur*, see Abraham E. Milgram, *Jewish Worship* (Philadelphia: Jewish Publication Society, 1971), Abraham Z. Idelsohn, *Jewish Liturgy and its Development* (New York: Dover Edition, 1995), and Ismar Elbogen, *Jewish Liturgy: A Comprehensive History* (Philadelphia: Jewish Publication Society, 1993).

10. "Jewish music" is heterogeneous, colored by regional, generational, and ideological forces. See Israel Adler, "Problems in the Study of Jewish Music," in *Proceedings of the World Congress of Jewish Music*, ed. Judith Cohen (Tel Aviv: Institute for the Translation of Hebrew Literature, 1982), pp. 15–27.

11. The European *Haskalah* (Enlightenment) of the eighteenth and nineteenth centuries, which favored the scientific-rationalism of the modern secular world, has had a lasting impact on Judaism. See Shmuel Feiner, *Haskalah and History: The Emergence of a Modern Jewish Historical Consciousness* (Oxford: Littman Library of Jewish Civilization, 2004), and Shmuel Feiner, *The Jewish Enlightenment* (Philadelphia: University of Pennsylvania Press, 2003).

12. See Ronald H. Isaacs, *Jewish Music: Its History, People, and Song* (Northvale, NJ: Jason Aronson, 1997).

13. Assimilation has been a major concern throughout Jewish history. For an exploration of the challenges of Jewish assimilation from ancient times to the present, see Menachem Mor, *Jewish Assimilation, Acculturation, and Accommodation* (Lanham, MD: University Press of America, 1991). For Jewish assimilation in the American context, see Neil M. Cowan and Ruth Schwartz Cowan, *Our Parents' Lives: Jewish Assimilation and Everyday Life* (New Brunswick, NJ: Rutgers University Press, 1996).

14. According to the Talmud, musical elements not of Jewish origin are *chukat hagoy* (custom of the gentile), and should not be allowed to enter the synagogue. See "Rabbinic Attitude to Music," in Israel Adler, *La pratique musicale savante dans quelques communaut 's juives en Europe aux XVIIé–XVIIIé siécles* (Paris, 1966), pp. 10–14.

15. See "The Music of the Hassidim: Melodies of Spiritual Ecstasy," in Heskes, *Passport to Jewish Music*, pp. 77–121.

16. Many of these Protestant-like synagogue songs were collected in "hymnals," to be used during services. For example, see *Union Songster: Songs and Prayers for Jewish Youth* (New York: Central Conference of American Rabbis, 1960).

17. Many scholars have addressed the lack of spiritual focus and increasing secularity of modern Jews. Among the most passionate on this issue was

Abraham Joshua Heschel (1907–72). See his books *Man's Quest for God: Studies in Prayer and Symbolism* (New York: Charles Scribner's Sons, 1954), and *The Sabbath* (New York: Farrar, Straus and Giroux, 1951).

18. Before the *Haskalah* (Enlightenment), notated Hebrew music was extremely rare. According to Israel Adler, "The total of such extant notations before 1800 and included in various collections thus far is hardly more than twenty." From Israel Adler, "The Notated Synagogue Chants of the 12th Century of Obidiah, the Norman Proselyte," in *Contributions to a Historical Study of Jewish Music*, ed. Eric Werner (New York: Ktav, 1976), p. 166.

19. See, for example, Esther Banbassa and Jean-Christophe Attias, *The Jews and Their Future: A Conversation on Judaism and Jewish Identity* (London: Zed Books, 2004), and Raymond P. Scheindlin, *A Short History of the Jewish People: From Legendary Times to Modern Statehood* (New York: Oxford University Press, 2000).

20. Even in the Reform movement, alteration of the prayer book has been a controversial issue. See, for example, Daniel Jeremy Silver, "On the Union Prayer Book," in *Central Conference of American Rabbis Journal* (January 1967): 11–19.

21. For a collection of articles discussing changes in synagogue music from antiquity to modern Israel, see Hanoch Avenary, *Encounters of East and West in Music* (Tel Aviv: Tel Aviv University Press, 1979).

22. See "Music in the Second Temple" and "Rabbinic Attitude Toward Music" in *Encyclopedia Judaica* (Jerusalem: Keter Publishing House, 1971), pp. 558–60, 566–67.

23. For example, *Lekhah Dodi* ("Come My Friend"), a popular *piyyut* (Jewish liturgical hymn), has well over 2,000 melodic variations. See Abraham Z. Idelsohn, *Jewish Music: Its Historical Development* (New York: Henry Holt and Co., 1929), p. 116, and "The Meaning of a Tune: The Sabbath Hymn *Lekhah dodi*," in Jeffery A. Summit, *The Lord's Song in a Strange Land: Music and Identity in Contemporary Jewish Worship* (New York: Oxford University Press, 2000), pp. 33–104.

24. Classical Rabbinic Judaism saw prayer as a religious obligation valid in itself, and cautioned against overemphasis on *kavvanah* (spontaneity; intentionality). For example, Rabbi Hayim of Volozhyn said, "It is better to pray gently and in a language of supplication than with *hitlahavut be-raash* (tumultuous enthusiasm)." From Louis Jacobs, *A Jewish Theology* (New York: Behrman House, 1973), pp. 189–90.

25. For more on the varied compositional approaches to liturgy, see "Changing Values in Synagogue Music," and "New Trends in Synagogue Music," in Irene Heskes, ed., *Studies in Jewish Music: The Collected Writings of A. W. Binder* (New York: Bloch Publishing Co., 1971), pp. 79-87, 230-241.

26. Ernest Bloch (1880–1977) is a composer widely lauded for his ability to both internalize and present liturgy with utmost skill and care. Of his

masterpiece "Avodath Hakodesh" ("Sacred Service"), Bloch remarked, "I have absorbed (the Shabbat morning liturgy) to the point that it has become mine and is as if it were the very expression of my soul." From Robert Strassburg, *Ernest Bloch: Voice in the Wilderness* (Los Angeles: Trident, 1977).

27. However, as Jeffery A. Summit contends, *nusach* (traditional chant) can be shaped by improvisation within the confines of the particular mode. See Summit's article "*Nusach* and Identity: The Contemporary Meaning of Traditional Prayer Modes," in *Music in American Religious Experience*, eds. Philip V. Bohlman, Edith L. Blumhofer, and Maria M. Chow (New York: Oxford University Press, 2006), pp. 271–86.

28. See Macy Nulman, "A Perception of the Prayer Modes in Musical and Rabbinic Sources," in *Musica Judaica: The Journal of The American Society for Jewish Music* VIII (1986–87): 45–58.

29. See the discussion of the *Missinai* ("From Sinai") tunes of the High Holidays in Stuart Weinberg Gershon, *Kol Nidrei: Its Origin, Development, and Significance* (Northvale, NJ: Jason Aronson, 1994), pp. 93–96, and Joseph A. Levine, *Synagogue Music in America* (Crown Point, IN: White Cliffs Media, 1989), pp. 44–54.

30. See Boaz Tarsi, "Tonality and Motivic Interrelationships in the Performance—Practice of Nusach," *Journal of Synagogue Music*, vol. XXI, no. 1, (1991): pp 5–27.

31. According to Jacob Neusner, "To be sure, lay people are as well educated as the rabbi in many ways. But in respect to the knowledge of Judaism, standards of literacy have so fallen that the rabbi now dominates in precisely the one area appropriate to his calling." From his book, *Israel in America: A Too Comfortable Exile* (Boston: Beacon Press, 1985), p. 23.

32. See Lazare Shaminsky, *Music of the Ghetto and the Bible* (New York: Bloch Publishing, 1934).

33. Joseph Yasser understood that pentatonic (five-note) scales emerged in ancient times, and evolved to seven and then twelve tones in the octave. See Joseph Yasser, *A Theory of Evolving Tonality* (Cambridge, MA: Da Capo Press, 1974).

34. For a comprehensive study of Bloch's life and works, see David Z. Kushner, *The Ernest Bloch Companion* (Westport, CT: Greenwood Press, 2001).

35. See "Israel's Choral Music," in *Studies in Jewish Music: Collected Writings of A. W. Binder*, ed. Irene Heskes (New York: Bloch Publishing, 1971), pp. 200–202.

36. Philip V. Bohlman refers to this simultaneous cultural preservation and change as *consolidation*: "The ethnic community must preserve certain facets of the pre-immigrant culture, yet change them to adapt to the new environment." From his book *"The Land Where Two Streams Flow": Music in the German-Jewish Community of Israel* (Chicago: University of Illinois Press, 1989), p. 111.

37. In anthropology, these directions of cultural change are *acculturation*, where the strength of a minority culture dictates the amount of change it undergoes, and *assimilation*, where the minority culture submits to dominant societal forces. See Conrad Philip Kottak, *Cultural Anthropology*, 10th ed. (New York: McGraw-Hill, 2004), pp. 140–42.

38. These two spiritual options are exemplified by traditional *halakhah* (Jewish law), which infuses God into all aspects of life, and Jewish humanism, which understands God—or a "God-concept"—as man's potential. To compare these views, see Joseph B. Soloveitchik, *Halakhic Man* (Philadelphia: Jewish Publication Society, 1983), and Erich Fromm, *You Shall Be As Gods: A Radical Interpretation of the Old Testament and Its Tradition* (New York: Holt, Rinehart, & Winston, 1966).

39. For more on the interrelation between Church and Synagogue music, see Eric Werner, *The Sacred Bridge: Liturgical Parallels in Synagogue and Early Church* (New York: Shocken Books, 1970).

40. See Gregory Wilbur, *The Music and Artistic Legacy of Johann Sebastian Bach* (Nashville, TN: Cumberland Publishing House, 2005).

41. See Eric Werner, *A Still Small Voice* (University Park: Pennsylvania State University Press, 1976).

42. For musical examples, see Velvel Pasternak, ed., *The Best of Hassidic Song Festivals* (New York: Tara Publications, 2006).

43. Secularity has come to characterize much of the modern Jewish experience, both in Israel and America. See, for example, Noah J. Efron, *Real Jews: Secular Versus Ultra-Orthodox and the Struggle for Jewish Identity in Israel* (New York: Basic Books, 2003), and Alan M. Dershowitz, *The Vanishing American Jew: In Search of Jewish Identity for the Next Century* (New York: Touchstone, 1998).

44. See Motti Regev and Edwin Seroussi, *Popular Music and National Culture in Israel* (Berkeley: University of California Press, 2004), and Zvi Keren, *Contemporary Israeli Music: Its Sources and Stylistic Development* (Ramat Gan, Israel: Bar Ilan University Press, 1980).

45. Thomas Merton (1915–58), an American Trappist monk, similarly warned against religious art that serves immediate aesthetic and participatory needs, but remains in the realm of the profane. He wrote, "Bad so-called sacred art constitutes a really grave spiritual problem…it affects us only slightly at first, but in the long run, the effect is grave." From Joan L. Roccasalvo, "The Sacred in Sacred Music," *America* (October 28, 1995): 19-21.

46. Both the traditional melody for *Etz Chayim* ("Tree of Life") and Nurit Hirsch's setting of *Oseh Shalom* ("Maker of Peace") are found in Charles Davidson, ed., *Gates of Song: Music for Shabbat* (New York: Transcontinental Music Publications, 1987).

47. For musical examples, see *Nigun Anthology—Volume 1: A Collection of Soulful Jewish Melodies* (Transcontinental Music Publications, 2004). See also

Louis Jacobs, *Hasidic Prayer* (New York: Shocken Books, 1973).

48. It is widely noted that the decrease in synagogue participation is related to the detachment of Jews from the spirit and meaning of liturgy. See, for example, Harold Kushner, *Who Needs God* (New York: Summit Books, 1989), pp. 143–62, and Seth Kadish, *Kavvana: Directing the Heart in Jewish Prayer* (Northvale, NJ: Jason Aronson, 1997).

CHAPTER 7

1. See Franz Rosenzweig, *The Star of Redemption* (New York: Holt, Rinehart & Winston, 1970).

2. Much of the sociology of religion explores the social preconditions for religious beliefs. See, for example, Peter L. Berger and Thomas Luckman, *The Social Construction of Reality: A Treatise in the Sociology of Knowledge* (New York: Anchor Books, 1967), Peter L. Berger, *The Sacred Canopy: Elements of a Sociological Theory of Religion* (New York: Anchor Books, 1969), and Robert N. Bellah, *Beyond Belief: Essays on Religion in a Post-Traditionalist World* (Berkeley: University of California Press, 1970).

3. Some scholars understand the sacred experience to be an authentic, nonrational, and mysterious encounter with the "Numinous," or "Holy Other." See, for example, Rudolf Otto, *The Idea of the Holy* (London: Oxford University Press, 1923), and Mircea Eliade, *The Sacred and Profane: The Nature of Religion* (New York: Harcourt, 1959).

4. Since the 1950s, religion in America has been colored largely by the individualism of spiritual seekers and their avoidance of tradition-oriented religious commitment. See Robert N. Bellah et al., *Habits of the Heart: Individualism and Commitment in American Life* (Berkeley: University of California Press, 1985), and Robert D. Putnam, *Bowling Alone: The Collapse and Revival of American Community* (New York: Simon & Shuster, 2000).

5. In the words of Lawrence A. Hoffman, traditional prayer is only meaningful when one "intends to appropriate it as his or her own." Quoted from his book *Beyond the Text: A Holistic Approach to Liturgy* (Bloomington: Indiana University Press, 1987), p. 7.

6. Saul L. Goodman claims that Jewish secularism emerged directly from the *Haskalah* (Enlightenment). See his book *The Faith of Secular Jews* (New York: Ktav Publishing House, 1976).

7. For a comprehensive look at the progressive beliefs and practices of liberal Judaism, see Eugene B. Borowitz, *Liberal Judaism* (New York: Union of American Hebrew Congregations Press, 1984).

8. Max I. Dimont characterizes Jewish survival as one of the most illogical in human history. See his book *Jews, God and History* (New York: Signet, 1964),

9. For more on the self-denial of assimilated modern Jews, see Eugene B. Borowitz's discussion of modern *marranos* (secretly practicing Jews) in his

book *The Masks Jews Wear: The Self-Deceptions of American Jewry* (New York: Simon & Schuster, 1980), pp. 26–41.

10. Jewish culture and music were largely homogeneous in the *shtetls* (small villages) of Eastern Europe. See Diane K. Roskies and David G. Roskies, *The Shtetl Book* (New York: Ktav Publishing House, 1975).

11. For more on the diversity of the American synagogue, see Jack Wertheimer, ed., *The American Synagogue: A Sanctuary Transformed* (Hanover, NH: Brandeis University Press, 1987).

12. The preservation of Jewish secular culture is a major concern in American Judaism. See Stephen J. Whitfield, *In Search of American Culture* (Hanover, NH: Brandeis University Press, 1999).

13. Traditionally, synagogue music was used to enhance the worship experience and help bring the congregation into the presence of God. See Judith K. Eisenstein, "The Mystical Strain in Jewish Liturgical Music," in *Sacred Sound: Music in Religious Thought and Practice*, ed. Joyce Irwin (Chico, CA: Scholar's Press, 1983), pp. 35–54.

14. For more on the spiritual efficacy of *hazzanut*, see Sharon Strassfeld and Michael Strassfeld, *The Second Jewish Catalog* (Philadelphia: Jewish Publication Society, 1976), pp. 368–76.

15. Similar cultural nostalgia has culminated in the revival of Eastern European *klezmer* (Jewish folk) music in the United States. See, for instance, "Klezmorim and Sephardim: The Jewish Music Revival," in Steven A. Marini, *Sacred Song in America: Religion, Music, and Public Culture* (Chicago: University of Illinois Press, 2003), pp. 130–59, and Seth Rogovoy, *The Essential Klezmer* (Chapel Hill, NC: Algonquin Books of Chapel Hill, 2000).

16. During the 1930s and 1940s, there was a surge of new synagogue compositions inspired by traditional synagogue modes and melodies, and which sought to distance the synagogue from the heavy influence of nineteenth century Protestant-like hymns. Composers such as Ernest Bloch, Herbert Fromm, and A. W. Binder were especially important in this regard. See Binder's essay, "New Trends in Synagogue Music," in *Studies in Jewish Music: Collected Writings of A. W. Binder*, ed. Irene Heskes (New York: Bloch Publishing, 1971), pp. 230–35.

17. Similar tensions between music and the sacred have occurred within Christian denominations, where many have noted the "dumbing down" of the musical content, the rapid disappearance of choirs, and the emergence of simplistic congregational singing. For more on sacred music in the Christian context, see Richard Viladesau, *Theology and the Arts: Encountering God through Music, Art and Rhetoric* (New York: Paulist Press, 2000).

18. In particular, the rise of denominationalism in America has given way to differing conceptions of "worship style." See Marc Lee Raphael, *Profiles in American Judaism: The Reform, Conservative, Orthodox, and Reconstructionist Traditions in Historical Perspective* (New York: Harper & Row, 1984).

19. See Rudolf Otto, *The Idea of the Holy* (London: Oxford University Press, 1923).

20. Cultural-secular Judaism has, since the advent of modernity, existed alongside religious Judaism as a means of preserving ethnic identity. For example, Theodor Herzl's (1860–1904) Political Zionism, and Mordecai Kaplan's (1881–1983) Reconstructionist Judaism were motivated largely by secular concerns. See David Ibry, *Exodus to Humanism: Jewish Identity Without Religion* (Amherst, NY: Prometheus Books, 1999), and Mordecai Kaplan, *Judaism as a Civilization: Toward a Reconstruction of American-Jewish Life* (New York: Macmillan Company, 1934).

21. In their book *Powers of Diaspora: Two Essays on the Relevance of Jewish Culture* (Minneapolis: University of Minnesota Press, 2002), Jonathan Boyarin and Danial Boyarin argue that the survival of Diaspora communities requires the strengthening of Jewish identity.

22. The various denominations of modern Judaism have constructed *siddurim* (prayer books) that approach the sacred in differing ways. See Lawrence A. Hoffman, *Beyond the Text: A Holistic Approach to Liturgy* (Bloomington: Indiana University Press, 1987).

23. For more on the weakening of the traditional mainstream and diversification of Jewish thought in the modern world, see Paul R. Mendes-Flohr and Jehuda Reinharz's anthology of historical essays, *The Jew in the Modern World: A Documentary History* (New York: Oxford University Press, 1980).

24. Abraham Joshua Heschel similarly cites this detachment from the sacred as a major problem in the contemporary cantorate. See his essay "The Vocation of the Cantor," in *The Insecurity of Freedom* (New York: Farrar, Straus and Giroux, 1966), pp. 242–53.

CHAPTER 8

1. One of the primary criticisms of modern American spirituality is that it lacks deep religious commitment, and is thus too transient, personalized, and "free-form" to foster connections with tradition. See Amanda Porterfield, *The Transformation of American Religion: The Story of a Late Twentieth-Century Awakening* (New York: Oxford University Press, 2001).

2. Numerous authors advocate approaching traditional Jewish devotion with both reverence and spontaneity. For example, see Lawrence A. Hoffman, *The Way Into Jewish Prayer* (Woodstock, VT: Jewish Lights Publishing, 2004), and Elie Munk, *World of Prayer* (Jerusalem: Feldheim Publishers, 1988).

3. The very act of *tefillah* (prayer) requires "building"—the daily repetition of the liturgy is intended to inspire and enhance spiritual development. As Evelyn Garfiel explains, "…prayers repeat their themes and their key phrases again and again until we begin to respond to their mood, until our natural preoccupation with our own worries, irritations, and limitations yields

to the larger outlook of the prayers." *The Service of the Heart: A Guide to the Jewish Prayer Book* (New York: Thomas Yoseloff, 1958), p. 106.

    4. For a brief and lucid discussion of the importance of Hebrew in both maintaining the integrity of Jewish prayer and inspiring *k'lal Yisrael* (Jewish solidarity), see "Must Prayer Be in Hebrew?" in Herman Wouk, *This Is My God* (New York: Doubleday, 1959), pp. 117–19.

    5. As Jakob J. Petuchowski explains in *Understanding Jewish Prayer* (New York: Ktav Publishing House, 1972), p. 46: "…let us bear in mind the genius of the Hebrew language which manages to convey a multitude of meanings in but a few well-chosen words. Each word comes with its own overtones and undertones, and numberless are the Bible verses which are open to more than one interpretation." For example, the opening of the *Shema*, the declaration of Jewish faith (*shema yisrael adonai eloheinu adonai echad*), has no less than thirty possible meanings, including "Hear, O Israel! The Lord our God is One Lord," and "Hear, O Israel! The Lord is our God, the Lord alone." From Louis Jacobs, *Principles of Jewish Faith* (New York: Basic Books, 1964), pp. 95–117.

    6. In particular, the Reform movement encourages Jews who cannot "read Hebrew with their eyes to offer it with their mouths." Richard N. Levy, *A Vision of Holiness: The Future of Reform Judaism* (New York: Union of Reform Judaism Press, 2005), p. 113. However, with this approach, prayers are often memorized from transliteration, which is not "universally accepted, accurate, easily comprehensible [or] consistent." Evelyn Garfiel, *The Service of the Heart: A Guide to the Jewish Prayer Book* (New York: Thomas Yoseloff, 1958), p. 223.

    7. For example, at some synagogues it is customary during the Friday evening Shabbat service to open the Ark holding the Torah for the chanting of *Shema* ("Hear, O Israel!") and *Alaynu* ("It Is Our Duty"), and all in attendance, including rabbi and cantor, turn and face the Ark.

    8. See "Individual Prayer within Communal Prayer," in Adin Steinsaltz, *A Guide to Jewish Prayer* (New York: Schocken, 2002), pp. 24–25.

    9. Facing the Ark should humble the cantor: "He does not stand before the ark as an artist in isolation, trying to demonstrate his skill or to display vocal feats. He stands before the ark not as an individual, but with the congregation. He must identify himself with the congregation. His task is to represent as well as to inspire the community." Abraham Joshua Heschel, *The Insecurity of Freedom* (New York: Farrar, Straus and Giroux, 1966), p. 244.

    10. For more on the historical development of the cantorate, see Leo Landman, *The Cantor: An Historical Perspective* (New York: Yeshiva University, 1972), and Mark Slobin, *Chosen Voices: The Story of the American Cantorate* (Chicago: University of Illinois Press, 1989).

    11. A problem in liberal Jewish worship is the pervasive notion that what was effective in the past—e.g., repetition of prayer and belief in the supernatural—is not compatible with post-Enlightenment Judaism. As such, various authors attempt to make prayer relevant for modern Jews. For a Conservative

Jewish perspective, see David Golinkin's essay, "Rediscovering the Art of Jewish Prayer," *United Synagogue Book Service* (December 7, 2004).

12. Interestingly, revival of the music of the past may function as "innovation" in the modern synagogue. As Mark Slobin suggests, "…tradition might itself be novel for a congregation that does not know the great works and melodies of the past." *Chosen Voices,* p. 185.

13. Orthodox Judaism maintains that a woman's voice in the synagogue is a sexual enticement (*kol be'ishah ervah*), and women are thus barred from the cantorate (Ber. 24a.). Concerning the modification of this prohibition, Baruch David Shreiber, an Orthodox commentator, asks, "How can we permit ourselves to change the age old structure of the synagogue service simply to satisfy neurotic outbursts of modernity, feminism, and the like?" From "The Woman's Voice in the Synagogue," *Essays of Jewish Music and Prayer*, ed. Macy Nulman (New York: Yeshiva University, 2005), p. 168. On the other hand, some feminist critique has emerged from within Orthodoxy. See, for instance, Tamar Ross, *Expanding the Palace of Torah: Orthodoxy and Feminism* (Hanover, NH: Brandeis University Press, 2004).

14. See Moshe Zemer, *Evolving Halakhah: A Progressive Approach to Traditional Law* (Woodstock, VT: Jewish Lights Publishing, 2003).

15. As Orthodox scholar Leo Landman states, "…in line with Christian acceptance of women as ministers, and as a complete break with Jewish tradition, the [Reform] School of Sacred Music has accepted women to train as cantors." *The Cantor: An Historical Perspective* (New York: Yeshiva University, 1972), p. 109.

16. The Conservative movement began ordaining female cantors in 1987. In total, the liberal denominations—Reform, Conservative, Reconstructionist—have ordained well over 200 women cantors. From Thomas Buergenthal and Courtney W. Howland, *Religious Fundamentalism and the Human Rights of Women* (New York: Palgrave Macmillan, 2001), p. 274.

17. See "1970s–1980s: New Trends, New Gender," in Slobin, *Chosen Voices,* pp. 113–34.

18. See Robert Donington, *Baroque Music, Style and Performance* (New York: W. W. Norton, 1982).

19. Cantorial settings of the liturgy, both in the past and within Orthodoxy today, were written for male voice (mostly tenor). See, for example, Gershon Ephrous, *Cantorial Anthology of Traditional and Modern Synagogue Music* (New York: Bloch Publishing, 2000).

20. See Samuel Rosenblatt, *Yossele Rosenblatt: The Story of His Life as Told by His Son* (New York: Farrar, Straus, and Young, 1954).

21. For example, Jack J. Cohen suggests that, as traditional faith is challenged in the postmodern world, a primary function of Jewish prayer is community preservation: "…it is through synagogue worship that the family ties can be strengthened and the family can sense its belonging to an inspiring tradition and to fellow Jews who share their ideals and their dreams." *Major*

Philosophers of Jewish Prayer in the Twentieth Century (New York: Fordham University Press, 2000), p. 208.

22. With the advent of the Jewish Diaspora, Temple sacrifice gave way to prayer as *the* mode of Jewish worship. With this transformation of worship modality came the need to organize essential prayers into a *siddur*. See Eliezer Berkovits, "From Temple to Synagogue and Back," *Judaism* (Fall 1959): 138–52. Further modifications of the *siddur* continue to this day with the emergence of denominations and other ideological shifts. See Stefan C. Reif, *Judaism and Hebrew Prayer: New Perspectives on Jewish Liturgical History* (New York: Cambridge University Press, 1993).

23. For more on the inner stream of prayer, see Joseph B. Soloveitchik, *Worship of the Heart: Essays on Jewish Prayer* (New York: Ktav Publishing, 2003).

24. This inner life of prayer is crucial. Lawrence A. Hoffman notes that, due largely to the fixity of the *siddur* (prayer book) and subsequent routines, "…most religious ritual in modern America is banal, poorly conceived, barely understood (even by those who direct it), and bordering on irrelevancy." *The Art of Public Worship* (Washington, DC: Westmore Press, 1998), p. ix. And, as Abraham Joshua Heschel wrote, "A revision of the prayer book will not solve the crisis of prayer. What we need is a revision of the soul, a new heart rather than a new text." *Man's Quest for God: Studies in Prayer and Symbolism* (New York: Charles Scribner's Sons, 1954), p. 83.

25. Much of this struggle with a God relationship stems from pre-Holocaust antitheological trends in American Judaism. See Robert G. Goldy, *The Emergence of Jewish Theology in America* (Bloomington: Indiana University Press, 1990). Likewise, the question of God's relevance in the postmodern world looms more broadly in mainline American Christianity. For example, see Thomas C. Reeves, *The Empty Church: The Suicide of Liberal Christianity* (New York: Free Press, 1996).

26. In particular, the Jews of Eastern Europe, due in part to their ghettoized communities, existed in a mainstream of *halakhah* (Jewish law). See, for example, Milton Metzler, *World of Our Fathers: The Jews of Eastern Europe* (New York: Dell Publishing, 1976).

27. For more on the importance of praying as a community, see Harold S. Kushner, *To Life: A Celebration of Jewish Being and Thinking* (New York: Warner Books, 1993), pp. 205–7, and Milton Steinberg, *Basic Judaism* (New York: Harcourt, Brace & World, 1947), pp. 117–18.

28. For more on the diversity of modern synagogue worship in America, see Jeffrey A. Summit, *The Lord's Song in a Strange Land: Music and Identity in Contemporary Jewish Worship* (New York: Oxford University Press, 2000).

29. The cantorial program at Hebrew Union College, Los Angeles, was founded in 1954.

30. Jacob Neusner concurs that rabbis in American liberal congregations are only required to know a little more than their largely liturgically illiterate

congregants. See his book *Israel in America: A Too-Comfortable Exile?* (Boston: Beacon Press, 1985), pp. 20–24.

31. For more on the rise and fall of the "star cantors" and their *hazzanut* in America, see "1880s–1940s: First and Second Generation Eastern Europeans," in Mark Slobin, *Chosen Voices: The Story of the American Cantorate* (Chicago: University of Illinois Press, 1989), pp. 51–77.

32. See David Saperstein, *Future of the Synagogue* (New York: Union of American Hebrew Congregations, 1976).

33. The Reform *siddur* was last updated with a "temporary" edition: *Gates of Prayer for Shabbat and Weekdays*, ed. Chaim Stern (New York: Central Conference of American Rabbis, 1994).

34. Many scholars have discussed the problems of reinvigorating Jewish identity in the postmodern world, and the constant temptations of assimilation and "radical choice" in contemporary Judaism. See, for example, Charles Selengut, ed., *Jewish Identity in the Post-Modern Age: Scholarly and Personal Reflections* (St. Paul, MN: Paragon House, 1999).

Selected Bibliography

"A Joyful Noise: Will much of Jewish music's beauty and history be lost as it adapts to the needs of the contemporary congregant?" *Jewish Journal of Greater Los Angeles* (May 12, 2000): 9–10.

Alperson, Philip, ed. *Musical Worlds: New Directions in the Philosophy of Music*. University Park: Pennsylvania State University Press, 1998.

Arendt, Hannah. *Eichmann in Jerusalem: A Report on the Banality of Evil*. New York: Penguin Classics Edition, 1994.

Avenary, Hanoch. *Encounters of East and West in Music*. Tel Aviv: Tel Aviv University Press, 1979.

Banbassa, Esther, and Jean-Christophe Attias. *The Jews and Their Future: A Conversation on Judaism and Jewish Identity*. London: Zed Books, 2004.

Bellah, Robert N. *Beyond Belief: Essays on Religion in a Post-Traditionalist World*. Berkeley: University of California Press, 1970.

———, et al. *Habits of the Heart: Individualism and Commitment in American Life*. Berkeley: University of California Press, 1985.

Benson, Herbert, and Miriam Z. Klipper. *The Relaxation Response*. New York: Avon Books, 1979.

Berger, Peter. *A Rumor of Angels: Modern Society and the Rediscovery of the Supernatural*. New York: Doubleday, 1969.

———. *The Sacred Canopy: Elements of a Sociological Theory of Religion*. New York: Anchor Books, 1969.

———, and Thomas Luckman. *The Social Construction of Reality: A Treatise in the Sociology of Knowledge*. New York: Anchor Books, 1967.

Berkovits, Eliezer. "From Temple to Synagogue and Back," *Judaism* (fall 1959): 138–52.

Birnbaum, Phillip. *Encyclopedia of Jewish Concepts*. New York: Hebrew Publishing Company, 1979.

Blackwell, Albert L. *The Sacred in Music*. Louisville: Westminster John Knox Press, 1999.

Bohlman, Philip V. *"The Land Where Two Streams Flow": Music in the German-Jewish Community of Israel*. Chicago: University of Illinois Press, 1989.

———, Edith L. Blumhofer, and Maria M. Chow, eds. *Music in American Religious Experience*. New York: Oxford University Press, 2006.

Bokser, Ben Zion, ed. *The Essential Writings of Abraham Isaac Kook*. Teaneck, NJ: Ben Yehudah Press, 2006.

Bolinger, Dwight L. *The Symbolism of Music*. Yellow Springs, OH: Antioch Press, 1941.

Borowitz, Eugene B., and Naomi Patz. *Explaining Reform Judaism*. West Orange, NJ: Behrman House, 1985.

Borowitz, Eugene B. *Liberal Judaism*. New York: Union of American Hebrew Congregations Press, 1984.

———. *The Masks Jews Wear: The Self-Deceptions of American Jewry*. New York: Simon & Shuster, 1980.

Boyarin, Jonathan, and Danial Boyarin. *Powers of Diaspora: Two Essays on the Relevance of Jewish Culture*. Minneapolis: University of Minnesota Press, 2002.

Buergenthal, Thomas, and Courtney W. Howland. *Religious Fundamentalism and the Human Rights of Women.* New York: Palgrave Macmillan, 2001.

Burstein, Abraham. *A New Concise Jewish Encyclopedia.* New York: Ktav Publishing, 1964.

Carlebach, Shlomo. *The Shlomo Carlebach Songbook.* New York: Zimrani Publishers, 1970.

Cimino, Richard, and Don Lattin. *Shopping for Faith: American Religion in the New Millennium.* San Francisco: Jossey-Bass, 1998.

Cohen, Jack J. *Major Philosophers of Jewish Prayer in the Twentieth Century.* New York: Fordham University Press, 2000.

Cohen, Judith, ed. *Proceedings of the World Congress of Jewish Music.* Tel Aviv: Institute for the Translation of Hebrew Literature, 1982.

Cohen, Ronald D. *Rainbow Quest: The Folk Music Revival and American Society, 1940–1970.* Amherst: University of Massachusetts Press, 2002.

Cowan, Neil M., and Ruth Schwartz Cowan. *Our Parents' Lives: Jewish Assimilation and Everyday Life.* New Brunswick, NJ: Rutgers University Press, 1996.

Dasilva, Fabio, Anthony Blasi, and David Dees. *The Sociology of Music.* Notre Dame: University of Notre Dame Press, 1984.

Davidson, Charles, ed. *Gates of Song: Music For Shabbat.* New York: Transcontinental Music Publications, 1987.

Davis, Cynthia. "The effects of music and basic relaxation instruction on pain and anxiety of women undergoing in-office gynecological procedures." *Journal of Music Therapy* 24, no. 4 (1992): 202–16.

Dershowitz, Alan M. *The Vanishing American Jew: In Search of Jewish Identity for the Next Century.* New York: Touchstone, 1998.

Diamant, Anita. *Choosing a Jewish Life: A Handbook for People Converting to Judaism and for Their Family and Friends.* New York: Schocken Books, 1998.

Dimont, Max I. *Jews, God and History.* New York: Signet, 1964.

Donin, Hayim Halevy. *To Pray as a Jew: A Guide to the Prayer Book and the Synagogue Service.* New York: Basic Books, 1991.

Donington, Robert. *Baroque Music, Style and Performance.* New York: W. W. Norton, 1982.

Dorff, Elliot N. *Prayer for the Perplexed.* Los Angeles: University of Judaism, 1982.

Dress, Steven W. "K-Date: The Embrace of Keva and Kavannah in the Conservative Synagogue." *United Synagogue Review* (spring/summer 2006): 24–26.

Edelman, Marsha Bryan. *Discovering Jewish Music.* Philadelphia: Jewish Publication Society, 2003.

Efron, Noah J. *Real Jews: Secular Versus Ultra-Orthodox and the Struggle for Jewish Identity in Israel.* New York: Basic Books, 2003.

Einstein, Albert. *The World as I See It.* New York: Philosophical Library, 1949.

Eisen, Arnold M. *Rethinking Modern Judaism: Ritual, Commandment, Community.* Chicago: University of Chicago Press, 1998.

———. *Taking Hold of Torah: Jewish Commitment and Community in America.* Bloomington: Indiana University Press, 1999.

Eisenstein, Judith Kaplan. *Heritage of Music.* New York: Union of American Hebrew Congregations, 1973.

———. "The Mystical Strain in Jewish Liturgical Music." In *Sacred Sound: Music in Religious Thought and Practice,* ed. Joyce Irwin. Chico, CA: Scholar's Press, 1983.

Elbogen, Ismar. *Jewish Liturgy: A Comprehensive History.* Philadelphia: Jewish Publication Society, 1993.

Eliade, Mircea. *The Sacred and Profane: The Nature of Religion.* New York: Harcourt, 1959.

Ellwood, Robert S. *Introducing Religion from Inside and Outside.* Upper Saddle River, NJ: Prentice Hall, 1983.

Ephrous, Gershon. *Cantorial Anthology of Traditional and Modern Synagogue Music.* New York: Bloch Publishing, 2000.

Ettin, Andrew Vogel. *Speaking Silences: Stillness and Voice in Modern Thought and Jewish Tradition.* Charlottesville: University of Virginia Press, 1994.

Feiner, Shmuel. *Haskalah and History: The Emergence of a Modern Jewish Historical Consciousness.* Oxford: Littman Library of Jewish Civilization, 2004.

———. *The Jewish Enlightenment.* Philadelphia: University of Pennsylvania Press, 2003.

Friedman, Daniel. *Jews without Judaism: Conversations with an Unconventional Rabbi.* Amherst, NY: Prometheus Books, 2002.

Fromm, Erich. *Psychoanalysis and Religion.* New York: Bantam Books, 1950.

———. *You Shall Be as Gods: A Radical Interpretation of the Old Testament and Its Tradition.* New York: Holt, Rinehart & Winston, 1966.

Fromm, Herbert. *On Jewish Music: A Composer's View.* New York: Bloch Publishing, 1978.

Galvin, Herman, and Stan Tamarkin. *The Yiddish Dictionary Sourcebook: A Transliterated Guide to the Yiddish Language.* New York: Ktav Publishing, 1986.

Garfiel, Evelyn. *The Service of the Heart: A Guide to the Jewish Prayer Book.* New York: Thomas Yoseloff, 1958.

Gates of Repentance: The New Union Prayer Book for the Days of Awe. New York: Central Conference of American Rabbis, 1978.

Gershon, Stuart Weinberg. *Kol Nidrei: Its Origin, Development, and Significance*. Northvale, NJ: Jason Aronson, 1994.

Gidal, Nachman T. *Jews in Germany: From Roman Times to the Weimar Republic*. Köhn, Germany: Könemann, 1998.

Gillman, Neil. *Conservative Judaism: The New Century*. West Orange, NJ: Behrman House, 1993.

Gilman, Sander L. *Jewish Self-Hatred: Anti-Semitism and the Hidden Language of the Jews*. Baltimore: Johns Hopkins University Press, 1986.

Glazer, Nathan. *American Judaism*. Chicago: University of Chicago Press, 1957.

Goldberg, Michael. *Why Should Jews Survive? Looking Past the Holocaust Toward a Jewish Future*. New York: Oxford University Press, 1995.

Goldy, Robert G. *The Emergence of Jewish Theology in America*. Bloomington: Indiana University Press, 1990

Golinkin, David. "Rediscovering the Art of Jewish Prayer." *United Synagogue Book Service* (December 7, 2004).

Goodman, Saul L. *The Faith of Secular Jews*. New York: Ktav Publishing House, 1976.

Hansen, William Lee. *The Atlantic Migration, 1607–1860: A History of the Continuous Settlement of the United States*. New York: Harper Torchlight, 1961.

———. *The Immigrant in American History*. Cambridge: Harvard University Press, 1940.

Hanser, Suzanne B. "Music therapy and stress reduction research." *Journal of Music Therapy* 12, no. 4 (1985): 193–206.

Harit-Manheimer, Aron, ed. *The Jewish Condition: Essays on Contemporary Judaism Honoring Rabbi Alexander M. Schindler*. New York: Union of American Hebrew Congregations, 1995.

Herberg, Will. *Protestant-Catholic-Jew: An Essay in American Religious Sociology*. Chicago: University of Chicago Press, 1955.

Herndon, Marcia, and Norma McLeod. *Music as Culture*. 2nd ed. Darby, PA: Norwood Editions, 1982.

Heschel, Abraham Joshua. *God in Search of Man: A Philosophy of Judaism*. New York: Harper & Row, 1955.

———. *The Insecurity of Freedom*. New York: Farrar, Straus and Giroux, 1966.

———. *Man's Quest for God: Studies in Prayer and Symbolism*. New York: Charles Scribner's Sons, 1954.

———. *The Sabbath*. New York: Farrar, Straus and Giroux, 1951.

Heskes, Irene. *Passport to Jewish Music: Its History, Traditions, and Culture*. New York: Tara Publications, 1994.

———, ed. *Studies in Jewish Music: Collected Writings of A. W. Binder*. New York: Bloch Publishing, 1971.

Hoffman, Lawrence A. *The Art of Public Worship*. Washington, DC: Westmore Press, 1998.

———. *Beyond the Text: A Holistic Approach to Liturgy*. Bloomington: Indiana University Press, 1987.

———. *The Way into Jewish Prayer*. Woodstock, VT: Jewish Lights Publishing, 2004.

Ibry, David. *Exodus to Humanism: Jewish Identity without Religion*. Amherst, NY: Prometheus Books, 1999.

Idelsohn, Abraham Z. *Jewish Liturgy and Its Development*. New York: Henry Holt, 1929.

Jacobs, Louis. *Hasidic Prayer*. New York: Shocken Books, 1973.

———. *A Jewish Theology*. New York: Behrman House, 1973.

———. *Principles of Jewish Faith*. New York: Basic Books, 1964.

James, William. *The Varieties of Religious Experience*. 5th printing. New York: Mentor, 1958.

Jick, Leon A. *The Americanization of the Synagogue, 1820–1870*. Hanover, NH: Brandeis University Press, 1976.

Johnson, Heather. "The New Cantor." *Reform Judaism* (winter 2003): 23–28, 44, 74–76.

Joselit, Jenna Weissman. *The Wonders of America: Reinventing Jewish Culture, 1880–1950*. New York: Henry Holt, 1994.

Kadish, Seth. *Kavvana: Directing the Heart in Jewish Prayer*. Northvale, NJ: Jason Aronson, 1997.

Kaplan, Dana. *Contemporary Debates in American Reform Judaism*. New York: Routledge, 2001.

Kaplan, Mordecai. *Judaism as a Civilization: Toward a Reconstruction of American-Jewish Life*. New York: Macmillan Company, 1934.

Keren, Zvi. *Contemporary Israeli Music: Its Sources and Stylistic Development*. Ramat Gan, Israel: Bar Ilan University Press, 1980.

King, Alan et al. *Matzo Balls for Breakfast, and Other Memories of Growing Up Jewish*. New York: Free Press, 2004.

Kirsch, Jonathan. *Moses: A Life*. New York: Ballantine Books, 1998.

Kottak, Conrad Philip. *Cultural Anthropology*. 10th ed. New York: McGraw-Hill, 2004.

Kushner, David Z. *The Ernest Bloch Companion*. Westport, CT: Greenwood Press, 2001.

Kushner, Harold S. *To Life: A Celebration of Jewish Being and Thinking*. New York: Warner Books, 1993.

———. *Who Needs God*. New York: Summit Books, 1989.

Landman, Leo. *The Cantor: An Historical Perspective*. New York: Yeshiva University, 1972.

Laswell, A. R. "The Effects of Music Assisted Relaxation on the Relaxation, Sleep Quality, and Daytime Sleepiness of Sheltered, Abused Women." Unpublished master's thesis, Florida State University, 2000.

Lazerwitz, Bernard, et al. *Jewish Choices: American Jewish Denominationalism*. New York: State University of New York Press, 1998.

Levine, Joseph A. *Synagogue Music in America*. Crown Point, IN: White Cliffs Media, 1989.

Levy, Richard N. *A Vision of Holiness: The Future of Reform Judaism*. New York: Union of Reform Judaism Press, 2005.

Mamet, David. *The Wicked Son: Anti-Semitism, Self-Hatred, and the Jews*. New York: Schocken, 2006.

Marcus, Jacob Rader, and Abraham J. Peck. *The American Rabbinate*. New York: Ktav Publishing House, 1985.

Marini, Steven A. *Sacred Song in America: Religion, Music, and Public Culture*. Chicago: University of Illinois Press, 2003.

Martin, Bernard. *Prayer in Judaism*. New York: Basic Books, 1968.

Matthews, Dale A., and Connie Clark. *The Faith Factor: Proof of the Healing Power of Prayer*. New York: Penguin, 1999.

Mendes-Flohr, Paul R., and Jehuda Reinharz. *The Jew in the Modern World: A Documentary History*. New York: Oxford University Press, 1980.

Metzler, Milton. *World of Our Fathers: The Jews of Eastern Europe*. New York: Dell Publishing, 1976.

Meyer, Leonard B. *Emotion and Meaning in Music*. Chicago: University of Chicago Press, 1958.

Meyer, Michael A. *Response to Modernity: A History of the Reform Movement in America*. Detroit: Wayne State University Press, 1995.

Milgram, Abraham E. *Jewish Worship*. Philadelphia: Jewish Publication Society, 1971.

Mor, Menachem. *Jewish Assimilation, Acculturation, and Accommodation*. Lanham, MD: University Press of America, 1991.

Munk, Elie. *World of Prayer*. Jerusalem: Feldheim Publishers, 1988.

Myron, Milton. *Assimilation in American Life: The Role of Race, Religion, and National Origins*. New York: Oxford University Press, 2002.

Netl, Bruno. *Theory and Method in Ethnomusicology*. New York: Macmillan, 1964.

Neusner, Jacob. *American Judaism: Adventures in Modernity*. Englewood Cliffs, NJ: Prentice Hall, 1972.

———. *Israel and Its Social Metaphors: Israel in the History of Jewish Thought*. Cambridge: Cambridge University Press, 1989.

———. *Israel in America: A Too Comfortable Exile?* Boston: Beacon Press, 1985.

———. *Judaism: The Basics*. New York: Routledge, 2006.

———. *The Midrash: An Introduction*. Northvale, NJ: Jason Aronson, 1990.

———, ed. *Understanding Jewish Theology: Classical Issues and Modern Perspectives*. New York: Ktav Publsihing, 1973.

———. *The Way of Torah: An Introduction to Judaism*. Belmont, CA: Dickenson Publishing, 1970.

Newton, Heber. *The Mysticism of Music*. New York: G. P. Putnam, 1915.

Nigun Anthology—Volume 1: A Collection of Soulful Jewish Melodies. Transcontinental Music Publications, 2004.

Nulman, Macy. *Concepts of Jewish Prayer and Music*. New York: Yeshiva University, 1985.

———. *Concise Encyclopedia of Jewish Music*. New York: McGraw-Hill, 1975.

———. *The Encyclopedia of Jewish Prayer*. Northvale, NJ: Jason Aronson, 1993.

———. "A Perception of the Prayer Modes in Musical and Rabbinic Sources." *Musica Judaica: The Journal of The American Society for Jewish Music* 8 (1986–87): 45–58.

Ockelford, Adam. *Repetition in Music: Theoretical and Metatheoretical Perspectives*. Burlington, VT: Ashgate Publishing, 2005.

Otto, Rudolf. *The Idea of the Holy*. London: Oxford University Press, 1923.

Pasternak, Velvel, ed. *The Best of Hassidic Song Festivals*. New York: Tara Publications, 2006.

Peters, Simi. *Learning to Read Midrash*. Jerusalem: Urim Publications, 2005.

Petuchowski, Jakob J. *Understanding Jewish Prayer*. New York: Ktav Publishing House, 1972.

Pogrebin, Abigail. *Stars of David: Prominent Jews Talk about Being Jewish*. New York: Broadway Books, 2005.

Porterfield, Amanda. *The Transformation of American Religion: The Story of a Late Twentieth-Century Awakening*. New York: Oxford University Press, 2001.

Putnam, Robert D. *Bowling Alone: The Collapse and Revival of American Community*. New York: Simon & Schuster, 2000.

Raphael, Marc Lee. *Profiles in American Judaism: The Reform, Conservative, Orthodox, and Reconstructionist Traditions in Historical Perspective*. New York: Harper & Row, 1984.

Reeves, Thomas C. *The Empty Church: The Suicide of Liberal Christianity*. New York: Free Press, 1996.

Regev, Motti, and Edwin Seroussi. *Popular Music and National Culture in Israel*. Berkeley: University of California Press, 2004.

Reif, Stefan C. *Judaism and Hebrew Prayer: New Perspectives on Jewish Liturgical History*. New York: Cambridge University Press, 1993.

Robb, S. L. et al., "The effects of music assisted relaxation on preoperative anxiety." *Journal of Music Therapy* 32, no. 1 (1995): 2–21.

Robinson, Jennifer. "The Expression and Arousal of Emotion in Music." In *Musical Worlds: New Directions in the Philosophy of Music*. Ed. Philip Alperson. University Park: Pennsylvania State University Press, 1998.

Roccasalvo, Joan L. "The Sacred in Sacred Music." *America* (October 28, 1995): 19-21.

Rogan, Eugene L. *Frontiers of the State in the Late Ottoman Empire: Transjordan, 1850–1921*. New York: Cambridge University Press, 2002.

Rogovoy, Seth. *The Essential Klezmer*. Chapel Hill, NC: Algonquin Books of Chapel Hill, 2000.

Rosenblatt, Samuel. *Yossele Rosenblatt: The Story of His Life as Told by His Son*. New York: Farrar, Straus and Young, 1954.

Rosenzweig, Franz. *The Star of Redemption*. New York: Holt, Rinehart & Winston, 1970.

Roskies, Diane K., and David G. Roskies. *The Shtetl Book*. New York: Ktav Publishing House, 1975.

Ross, Tamar. *Expanding the Palace of Torah: Orthodoxy and Feminism*. Hanover, NH: Brandeis University Press, 2004.

Rosten, Leo. *The Joys of Yiddish*. New York: McGraw-Hill, 1968.

Rubin, Barry. *Assimilation and its Discontents*. New York: Times Books, 1995.

Sacks, Jonathan. www.chiefrabbi.org/articles/ljnjt/yomkippur.htm., accessed January 12, 2007.

Saperstein, David. *Future of the Synagogue*. New York: Union of American Hebrew Congregations, 1976.

Sarna, Jonathan D. "The Question of Music in American Judaism." *American Jewish History* (June 2003): 195–204.

Satlow, Michael L. "Defining Judaism: Accounting for 'Religions' in the Study of Religion." *Journal of the American Academy of Religion* 74, no. 4 (2006): 837–860.

Savage, Roger. W. H. "Music and Cultural Imagination." In *Selected Reports in Ethnomusicology*, Vol. X. Los Angeles: UCLA Department of Ethnomusicology, 1994.

Scheindlin, Raymond P. *A Short History of the Jewish People: From Legendary Times to Modern Statehood*. New York: Oxford University Press, 2000.

Shaminsky, Lazare. *Music of the Ghetto and the Bible*. New York: Bloch Publishing, 1934.

Shapiro, Mark Dov. *Gates of Shabbat: A Guide for Observing Shabbat*. New York, Central Conference of American Rabbis Press, 1996.

Shinan, Avigdor. *The World of the Aggadah*. Tel Aviv: Mod Books, 1997.

Silver, Daniel Jeremy. "On the Union Prayer Book." *Central Conference of American Rabbis Journal* (January 1967): 11–19.

Slobin, Mark. *Chosen Voices: The Story of the American Cantorate*. Chicago: University of Illinois Press, 2002.

Sohngen, Oskar. "Music and Theology: A Systematic Approach." In *Sacred Sound: Music in Religious Thought and Practice*, ed. Joyce Irwin. Chico, CA: Scholars Press, 1983. 1–20.

Solomon, Norman. *Judaism: A Very Short Introduction*. New York: Oxford University Press, 1996.

Soloveitchik, Joseph B. *Halakhic Man*. Philadelphia: Jewish Publication Society, 1983.

———. *Worship of the Heart: Essays on Jewish Prayer*. New York: Ktav Publishing, 2003.

Steinberg, Milton. *Basic Judaism*. New York: Harcourt, Brace & World, 1947.

Steinsaltz, Adin. *A Guide to Jewish Prayer*. New York: Schocken, 2002.

Stern, Chaim, ed. *Gates of Prayer for Shabbat and Weekdays*. New York: Central Conference of American Rabbis, 1994.

Stokes, Martin, ed. *Ethnicity, Identity and Music: The Musical Construction of Place*. New York: Berg Publishers, 1997.

Stone, Abraham. "Voice Level in Tefillah." In *Essays of Jewish Music and Prayer*, ed. Macy Nulman. New York: Yeshiva University, 2005.

Strassburg, Robert. *Ernest Bloch: Voice in the Wilderness*. Los Angeles: Trident, 1977.

Strassfeld, Sharon and Michael Strassfeld. *The Second Jewish Catalog*. Philadelphia: Jewish Publication Society, 1976.

Summit, Jeffery A. *The Lord's Song in a Strange Land: Music and Identity in Contemporary Jewish Worship*. New York: Oxford University Press, 2000.

Tanakh: The Holy Scriptures. Philadelphia: Jewish Publication Society, 1985.

Telushkin, Joseph. *Jewish Literacy*. New York: William Morrow, 1991.

Temkin, Shefton D. *Creating American Reform Judaism: The Life and Times of Isaac Mayer Wise*. Oxford: Littman Library of Jewish Civilization, 1998.

Union Songster: Songs and Prayers for Jewish Youth. New York: Central Conference of American Rabbis, 1960.

Viladesau, Richard. *Theology and the Arts: Encountering God through Music, Art and Rhetoric*. New York: Paulist Press, 2000.

Werner, Eric, ed. *Contributions to a Historical Study of Jewish Music*. New York: Ktav, 1976.

———. *From Generation to Generation: Studies on Jewish Musical Tradition*. New York: American Conference of Cantors, 1967.

———. *The Sacred Bridge: Liturgical Parallels in Synagogue and Early Church*. New York: Schocken Books, 1970.

———. *A Still Small Voice*. University Park: Pennsylvania State University Press, 1976.

Wertheimer, Jack, ed. *The American Synagogue: A Sanctuary Transformed*. Hanover, NH: Brandeis University Press, 1995.

Whitfield, Stephen J. *In Search of American Culture*. Hanover, NH: Brandeis University Press, 1999.

Wilbur, Gregory. *The Music and Artistic Legacy of Johann Sebastian Bach*. Nashville, TN: Cumberland Publishing House, 2005.

Wouk, Herman. *This Is My God*. New York: Doubleday, 1959.

Wuthnow, Robert. *After Heaven: Spirituality in America Since the 1950s*. Berkley: University of California Press, 1998.

———. *Christianity in the 21st Century: Reflections on the Challenges Ahead*. New York: Oxford University Press, 1993.

Yasser, Joseph. *A Theory of Evolving Tonality*. Cambridge: Da Capo Press, 1974.

Zemer, Moshe. *Evolving Halakhah: A Progressive Approach to Traditional Law*. Woodstock, VT: Jewish Lights Publishing, 2003.

Index

A

Abraham, 51
Addison, Joseph, xi
Adler, Israel, 133 n. 18
Adon Olam, 22
Aggadah, 58
Ahavah Rabbah, 47
Amen, xiv, 32
American Judaism, ix, 4–5, 11, 39–40. See also Assimilation, Jewish Ethnicity, Jewish identity
    continuity and fragmentation of, ix, 20, 24, 27, 29, 31, 64
    denominationalism in, 11, 127 n. 3
    the seeker in, 75–77
    universalism in, 46
American Religion, viii, ix, xi, 4–5, 138 n. 1, 141 n. 24
Amidah, 72
Am Yisrael, 4
Ark, 10, 41, 55, 90–91, 139 n. 9
Ashkenazi, 19, 59, 64
Ashrei, 31
Assimilation, 3, 11, 12, 19, 40, 51, 59, 85. See also Eric Werner
    active and passive, viii–ix, 52–53, 59–62, 63, 67–68, 78
Auschwitz, 51
Avodath Hakodesh, 66
Avot, 31
Az Yashir, xv

B

Baal Shem Tov, 4
Ba'al tefillah, 21, 22, 24, 41
Bach, Johann Sebastian, 69, 95–96
Bar'chu, 27
Bashanah, 70
Beerman, Leonard I., 37
Beethoven, Ludwig van, xi, xvi
Beimel, Jacob, 5
Bellah, Robert, 16
Berachot, 32
Berger, Peter, xi–xiii
Bima, 21, 29, 78
Binder, Abraham Wolf, 67, 126 n. 29
Birnbaum, A. B., 28, 125 n. 22
Bloch, Ernest, 66, 133 n. 26, 137 n. 16
Bohlman, Philip V., 134 n. 36
Bolinger, Dwight L., 7
Borge, Victor, xiv
Borowitz, Eugene B., 136 n. 9
Bronx, 35
Bruch, Max, 8
Buber, Martin, 10

C

Cantillation, 4, 104
Cantor (cantorate), 9–17, 33, 36–37, 42, 54, 55, 59, 90–91, 92, 103. See also *Hazzan*
    role of, 10–17, 23, 63, 81, 97, 101
    "conquering cantor," 13
    and choir, 25–26, 27

159

and humility, 10, 12–13, 17
improvisation of, 91
and performance, 79–81, 91
training of, vii, 37–38, 81, 102–5
women as, 93–97, 140 n. 13, 140 n. 16
Carlebach, Shlomo, 15
Cello, 8
Central Conference of American Rabbis, 104
Choir, 25–26, 27, 80, 81
Chol, 42
Christianity, 4
Chukat Hagoy, 87
Cincinnati, 36
Cohen, Jack J., 140 n. 21
Congregational singing, 13–16, 19, 22–26, 43, 44, 53–54, 80–81
and choir, 27, 80
and "just" listening 54
in the nineteenth century, 26–28
Conservative Judaism, 28–29, 41, 44, 59
women in, 93–95

D

Daven (*Davening, Davener*) 13, 16, 19, 20–23, 42, 43, 52, 55, 77, 79–81, 87, 95. See also *Tefillah*; Prayer
and *hazzanut*, 23–26, 52–53
variety of, 28–29
David, (King), xvi
Depression, the, 35
Desecularization, 69. See also Secular
Diaspora, 51, 52, 59, 61, 66, 77, 82, 121 n. 8
Dimont, Max I, 136 n. 8
Divine, the, xiv, 5, 82, 122 n. 6. See also *Shekhinah*

E

Echad Eloheinu, 31
Edelman, Marsha Bryan, 128 n. 9
Eichmann, Adolf, xii
Eine Kleine Nachtmusik, 31

Ein Kamokha, 27
Ein Kelohaynu, 22
Einstein, Alfred, 84
Eisen, Arnold, 129 n. 15
El Adon, 22
Ellwood, Robert S., xiv
Enlightenment, 82. See also *Haskalah*
Erev Shel Shoshanim, 31
Ethnomusicology, 3, 134 n. 36
Etz Chayim, 71

F

French, 69
Friedman, Daniel, 130 n. 22
Friedman, Debbie, 14
Friedman, Lev, 16
Fromm, Erich, 11
Fromm, Herbert, 126 n. 29, 137 n. 16

G

Garfiel, Evelyn, 138 n. 3
Gates of Prayer, 97–102
Gemarah, xv
Germany, 19. See also Reform Judaism
Get, 41
Ghetto, 25–26
Glazer, Nathan, 4
Goldfarb, Israel, 31
Goodman, Saul L., 136 n. 6

H

Halakhah, 20, 61, 94
Hansen, William Lee, 127 n.5
Hasidic Song Festival, 70, 73
Hasidism (Hasidic), 4, 6, 11, 47, 70, 72
Haskalah, 59
Havdalah, 32
Hazzan, 21, 22, 23–26, 29, 42, 52–53, 55, 78, 79–81, 94, 95–97, 103. See also Cantor
Hazzanut, 4, 23, 24, 25, 27, 44–45, 73, 79–80, 93, 94, 95–97, 103–104

Hebrew, ix, 15, 20, 24, 42, 44, 55, 66, 89–90, 104, 135 n. 5
  instruction in, vii, 90
Hebrew Union College, 36–37, 46–47, 141 n. 29
Heraclitus, 1
Herberg, Will, 129 n. 16
Herzl, Theodor, 138 n. 20
Heschel, Abraham Joshua, 12–13, 15–16, 124 n. 7, 133 n. 17, 138 n. 24, 141 n. 24
High Holy Days, 10, 61
High Priest, 63
Hillel, 38
Hirsch, Nurit, 71, 135 n. 46
Hishtapkhut hanefesh, 12
Hitler, Adolf, 51
Hoffman, Lawrence A., 136 n. 5, 141 n. 24
Holocaust, xii, 51
Homo ludens, xii. See also Signal of Transcendence
Humanitas, xii, xvii. See also Signal of Transcendence
Humor, xii. See also Signal of Transcendence
  in music, xiv
Huxley, Aldous, xi

I

Intermarriage, 40, 126–7 n. 6
Israel, musical influence of, 66–73

J

James, William, 6
Jewish Ethnicity, 4–5, 77. See also American Judaism; Jewish identity
Jewish Identity, 7, 10, 12, 40, 42–43, 44, 45, 49, 51, 75, 77–79, 129 n. 15
  and the family, 121 n. 8
Jewishness, 15
Jewish Studies, vii–viii
Justice, xii. See also Signal of Transcendence
  in music, xiv

K

Kabbalat Shabbat, 31
Kaddish, 31
Kahal, 23, 31, 55
Kaplan, Mordecai, 138 n. 20
Kashrut, 48
Kavvanah, ix, 10–11, 12, 32, 55, 123 n. 21, 131 n. 6, 133 n. 24. See also *Keva*
Kedushah, 22, 27, 31
Keva, ix, 11, 131 n. 6. See also *Kavvanah*
Kippah, 41
Klepper, Jeff, 14
Kodesh, 42
Kol Nidre, 7–9, 48. See also Max Bruch
  "*Kol Nidre* Jews," 8
Kook, Abraham Isaac, 127 n. 36
Kvod hatzibbur, 94

L

Lenau, Nikolaus, 8
Leo Baeck Temple, viii, 36–37, 41, 45–46, 59
Levite, 63
Lewandowski, Louis, 26–27, 29
Listening, 43, 54–55, 57, 80
Los Angeles, vii, viii, 36–37, 46, 87

M

Ma'ariv, 65, 79–80
Manhattan School of Music, 36
Mathews, Dale, xvi
Ma Tovu, 22
"May the Words," 71
Mechitzah, 94
Mencken, H. L., xi
Merton, Thomas, 14, 135 n. 45
Midrash, 58, 62–63

Minhag, 94
Minyan, 20
Mishnah, xv
Mozart, Amadeus, 31
Music. See also Synagogue song
   and culture, 3, 24
   and emotion, xv–xvi, 3, 5–8, 10, 13, 48
   as essential, xiii, 1, 3
   ethnicity in, 3, 17, 20, 134 n. 36
   healing power of, xvi–xvii
   humor in, xiv
   and identity, 10, 48, 53, 59
   justice in, xiv
   and language, xv, 4, 7, 57
   and medicine, xvi–xvii
   and mood, 8, 65
   music–less–ness, xiii
   as nonrational, 5–7
   nostalgia and, 7, 9, 11–12, 48
   order in, xiii–xiv
   as playful, xiv
   in religion, xi, xiv, xv, 1, 5
   repetition in, 7, 43, 46–47, 90
   and text, vii, xv, 6–7, 16–17, 57–59, 64
Mysterium tremendum, 17

N

Neo–Orthodox Judaism, 93–94
Neusner, Jacob, 11–12, 127 n. 3, 134 n. 31, 141 n. 30
New York City, 35–36, 41, 87
Niggun, 6, 72. See also Hasidism
Nusach, viii–ix, 4, 15, 21, 24, 31, 64–65, 73, 93, 104, 128 n. 9, 130 n. 3, 134 n. 27

O

Orchestra, 6
Order, xii. See also Signal of Transcendence
   in music, xiii–xiv, 27
Orthodox Judaism, ix, 16, 22, 35, 42, 43, 45, 59, 63, 79, 81, 87, 128 n. 8
   women in, 93–95, 140 n. 13

Oseh Shalom, 71
Otto, Rudolf, 5

P

Petuchowski, Jakob, 129 n. 14, 139 n. 5
Piano, vii, 35
Pirke Avot, 38
Postmodernity, ix, 1
Prayer, ix, 11–12, 42, 75, 76–77, 79. See *Tefillah*; *Daven*
   in American Judaism, 12, 17, 101–102
   and community, 140 n. 21
   in English, 89–90
   and nonbelievers, 76, 129 n. 13
   relevance of, viii, 28, 81–8
Prayer book, 41, 77, 83, 97–102. See also *Siddur*
Pulpit, fragmentation of, 55

R

Rabbi, 41, 55, 58, 63, 91, 94, 101, 134 n. 31
Rabbinical school, 47
Reform Judaism, ix, 22, 24–25, 59, 91, 96
   in America, 25, 29–30, 42, 43–44, 45, 47, 48, 63, 80, 128 n. 8
   in Germany, 19, 27–28, 61
   women in, 93–95
Rosenblatt, Yossele, 96, 125 n. 13
Rosenzweig, Franz, 75
Rosh Hashanah, 9. See also High Holy Days; *Yamim Nora'im*

S

Sabbath (Shabbat), 12, 32, 65, 79, 80, 87–88, 89
Sacks, Sir Jonathan, xv
Salanter Yeshiva, 35
Saminsky, Lazare, 66
Saul (King), xvi
Schreiber, Baruch David, 140 n. 13
Second Temple, 60, 63

Secular (secularization), ix, xi, 67
  in Judaism, 8, 15–16, 30, 32, 40, 45, 55, 60, 61, 67, 68–69, 70, 72–73, 77–79, 82, 83, 84–85, 126 n. 24
Separateness, 78
Shalom Aleichem, 31
Sharlin, William, vii–ix, 33–49, 127 n. 2, 129 n.18
Shekhinah, 4, 6, 10–11. See also Divine
Sheliach Tzibbur, 10, 21, 24, 31, 94
Shtibel, 20
Shuckling, 20
Shul, 20, 21, 42, 79, 87
Sh'ma Yisrael, 27
Siddur, 21, 55. See also Prayer book
  as "anchor," 57–59, 62, 99–100, 102
Signals of Transcendence, xi. See also Peter Berger
  categories of, xii–xiii
  music as, xiii–xvii
Sinai, 57
Slobin, Mark, 140 n. 12
Stokes, Martin, 3
Sulzer, Solomon, 26–27, 29, 125 n. 16
Summer camps, 14, 30
Summit, Jeremy A., 134 n. 27
Synagogue, viii, ix,
Synagogue song, xv, 1, 3, 46, 57–58, 83–85. See also Music
  active and passive assimilation in, viii–ix, 52–53, 59–62, 63, 67–68, 78
  in America, 11–12, 14–15, 45
  composers of, 51–53, 64, 66–67
  and culture, 24,79–81
  diversity of, viii, 51–53, 58–59, 61–62, 63, 64, 78, 81, 92–93
  in Eastern Europe, 52–53
  insiders and outsiders in, 51–53, 105
  importance of, vii–viii, xv, 5
  Israel's relationship to, 66–73
  and Jewish identity, 7
  mainstream in, 59–60, 63, 67, 70, 83
  pop music in, 30, 43, 47–48, 53, 70–71, 79, 128 n. 12
  static and dynamic, 57–59

T

Talmud, 61
Tefillah, 16, 19, 20, 21, 22, 28, 29, 30, 31, 32, 42, 43–44, 46, 52, 64–65, 85, 95,101, 131 n. 3. See also *Daven*; *Prayer*
Torah, 41, 44, 57, 77, 131 n. 1
True believer, 75
Tzadik, 10

U

Universalism, 45–46

V

Varieties of Religious Experience, 6
"Vocation of the Cantor," 12–13

W

Washington Heights, 35
Weinberg, Jacob, 66
Werner, Eric, viii, 36, 69
"Wholly Other," 5–6. See also Rudolf Otto

Y

Yamim Nora'im, 21–22. See also High Holy Days
Yasser, Joseph, 66, 134 n. 33
Yeshiva, 35, 37, 39, 63
Yeshiva D'Harlem, 35
Yeshiva University High School, 35, 36
Yiddish, 39
Yom Kippur, 8–9, 47–48. See also High Holy Days; *Yamim Nora'im*

Z

Zalman, Shneur, 6
Zmirot, 31